Our Own Worst Enemy as Protector of Ourselves

Stereotypes, Schemas, and Typifications as Integral Elements in the Persuasive Process

Byron B. Renz

UNIVERSITY PRESS OF AMERICA,® INC.
Lanham • Boulder • New York • Toronto • Plymouth, UK

Copyright © 2010 by
University Press of America,® Inc.
4501 Forbes Boulevard
Suite 200
Lanham, Maryland 20706
UPA Acquisitions Department (301) 459-3366

Estover Road
Plymouth PL6 7PY
United Kingdom

British Library Cataloging in Publication Information Available

Library of Congress Control Number: 2009931143
ISBN: 978-0-7618-4704-5 (paperback : paper)
eISBN: 978-0-7618-4705-2

To my parents, Ben and Florence Renz

Who encouraged intellectualism, creativity, curiosity, and the will to take the image of curious inquiry and to communicate it in an intellectual and creative context.

Even if you persuade me, you won't persuade me.

Aristophanes *Frogs* 405 B.C.

Contents

Contents

Figures

Introduction: The Function of Persuasion in Propaganda

"That's nothing but propaganda," he said, and with that summary dismissal, the speaker went on to assert his own opinion on the issue. From an objective perspective, his opinion very likely landed in the same trash can as the statement described as "nothing but propaganda." Propaganda is often promulgated in superlative attack language, with the immediate conviction that the attacker is trying to thrust a sword into the body of beliefs and values of the recipient of the persuasive message. Or, propaganda may be subtle, creeping in the back door so as not to be noticed. We might also envision persuasive messages as poison-tipped arrows—tipped with the poison of value-laden propaganda—that impinge on our consciousness.

The common perception of what Ellul calls *sociological* propaganda is that propaganda is a diabolical scheme by an enemy to destroy one's value system, which is the bedrock of one's society (Ellul, *Propaganda*, 62-71). With the bedrock undermined, the superstructure crumbles. Of course, propaganda may have more limited strategic objectives (to accomplish short-range rather than long-range objectives), as is often the case with military psychological operations during wartime. But, our primary concern in this book is with the use of persuasive messages on a universal basis and with an indefinite endpoint. Our primary focus is on the influence on values and beliefs more than immediate strategic advantage on the battlefield; fundamental principles of propaganda, however, may be applied in both instances. Nevertheless, the battle of cultures (based on different value systems) has been with us from the beginning of human history.

Therefore, propaganda as "our own worst enemy" is thought of as consisting of several venomous components. Propaganda assumes that communication is cynically manipulated to undermine the treasured values of the recipient; therefore, it is evil. Propaganda assumes that statements consist of intentional lies; therefore it is evil. Propaganda consists of intentional deception through the omission of details that would allow for the creation of a full-fledged, objective, truthful story; therefore, because propaganda frequently includes selective omission of details, it is evil. Propaganda, as a kind of space junk of the electromagnetic communication channels, constitutes a physical and psychological pollution of our communication channels. The destructive debris decreases our ability to understand ideas and positions on issues accurately and to gain meaningful knowledge. Propaganda sneakily hides a sinister intent to injure the recipient of the communication; therefore, it is evil.

Considered collectively, these elements give us a picture of an evil entity, hypnotically manipulating the recipient of propaganda messages, like Svengali, in George du Maurier's 1894 novel *Trilby,* who exercises an unseen power over his helpless victim, Trilby. Propaganda, too, is perceived of as having a hypnotic power over the recipient of the messages. Maurier's *Trilby* captures the essence of the belief regarding an opponent's propaganda. It is sinister; it is controlling; it is self-centered; it is cynical; it is derisive; it is full of malice. Svengali is the prototype of our current image of the propagandist. Invective, lies, pernicious distortion of information—these are often viewed as the worst form of pollution, that is, "our own worst enemy."

Propaganda is communication; therefore, it requires a receiver as well as a sender. And, the response of the receiver is the second part of the propaganda equation. The receiver has a typical response to the sent message—a defensive response to the first-strike attack of the sender. A defensive wall immediately springs up around the receiver of the persuasive message, and a counterattack (either actual or mental) is launched against the encoded values of the propagandist. The defensive wall is both protection of one's own value system and a staging ground for an ideational counterattack. Therefore, propaganda involves a two-step, interactive process between a sender and a receiver. Attack and defense constitute the two components of a propaganda message.

The defensive step in the propaganda attack-and-defense capsule might be envisioned as the outer wall of a medieval castle. The wall springs up from our adaptive unconscious, where the value and belief packets are stored as schemas, typifications, and stereotypes. The wall rises instantaneously and without conscious control. In most instances, we aren't even aware that we are in an attack-and-defense mode within a propaganda capsule. We are unconsciously using the idea construction and its associated emotion through the defensive form of the shield and the offensive counterattacking mechanism of the sword in an effort to protect ourselves and to bring understanding of the world into compliance with the "truth," that is, with our individual perception of how things should be. Therefore, the first defensive action is to raise the wall of our medieval castle (which occurs spontaneously and unconsciously). The second step is to bring our archers or riflemen into the crenels of the wall, the carved out areas that separate the merlons, the high segments of a battlement. From there, protected by the defensive wall, the reciprocator in the propaganda capsule can fire his missiles—his ideas and emotions that are inconsistent with the form assumed by the attacker. The conscious response, either physical or mental, is directed by the pattern of the schemas, but the responder is seldom aware of the connection between the two. All that he knows is that he is defending his beliefs and, thus, reinforcing the group belief structure of which he is a part (capitalism, Catholicism, etc.). That support of the group provides psychological comfort for the propaganda recipient, a feeling of satisfaction as one settles, psychologically, into the comforting and accepting part of one's group. So, as we launch a counterattack on the propagandist's message, we are both destroying "untruth" and revealing a "truer," more refined and sophisticated reality of world dynamics.

To the extent that we use propaganda to encourage the world—or a particular society in it—to accept the "correct" interpretation of the universe, we are shining the light of "truth" on the world and encouraging the world to accept our beliefs and values as the foundation for their societies. Once the receiver, who is "correcting" his value/belief system, has built a value/belief foundation, he would then be able to build a superstructure on that foundation that would reflect the new belief and value system. This would bring the two parties in the dyad into essential harmony with each other. The potential for conflict is reduced considerably between societies that have similar value/belief systems. Therefore, to the extent that the society with the "truth" prevails, those societies, as well as the persuaded societies, are protectors of their own self-interests and, therefore, "protector(s) of [themselves] ourselves."

Yet, it might be argued that with the increased intercultural interaction as a result of globalization and advanced and relatively inexpensive transportation systems, belief and value systems may converge automatically as people interact in response to common economic expectations. There is, however, no requirement that world commerce need be carried out by societies with similar political systems or value/belief systems. In fact, one of the reasons that some endogenous population groups within larger nation-states seek autonomy or separate nationhood is that they are seeking freedom to build their societal superstructure on their own value and belief systems. Thus, the number of political entities based on particular value systems is increasing.

There is no need to provide exhaustive examples of value and belief sets that represent the numerous self-interests of a rapidly multiplying world population. Values come in many belief sets—economic, political, religious, sociological, and ethnic, among others. But, one more example should suffice to make the point that values are diverging as groups holding these values grow in number, seek political autonomy, and migrate around the world.

The Pollyannas among us might say that the ethnic groups (the races) are converging, and, as that happens, our values are bound to converge, too, automatically, without our having to do anything about it. Our view is that human evolution is over. Ever since Homo sapiens emerged on earth, they have built their culture and society with the same body and brain. If mankind were automatically converging toward harmony, then the case for proactive and reactive propaganda would diminish in importance. Harmony would allow for an automatic convergence of beliefs and values; so, why bother with propaganda? The ethnic example, of course, is just one of many that might represent differing value and belief systems. Socioeconomic differences would be another, but one example should make the point.

Actually, a number of studies in the early twenty-first century suggest that human evolution is far from over and that humans are actually changing faster than ever (McAuliff, 2009 March, 51). These researchers have found an " . . . abundance of recent adaptive mutations etched in the human genome; even more shocking, these mutations seem to be piling up faster and ever faster, like an avalanche" (Ibid.).

The mutations relate to essential functions of bodily organs—the brain, the digestive system, life span, immunity to pathogens, sperm production, and bones—all essential aspects of human functioning. But, the most significant finding for those concerned about persuasive messages in relation to ethnic value systems is that "Many of these DNA variants are unique to their continent of origin, with provocative implication" (Ibid.). "We are getting less alike, not merging into a single mixed humanity," according to University of Utah anthropologist Henry Harpending (quoted in McAuliff, 51).

If, indeed, humanity is continuing to evolve into increasingly diverse variants, it remains just as important now, as it has been in the past, that we pay careful attention to propaganda and the way that persuasion is used. As the world's population increases, with ever more belief systems making up the aggregate whole of a society, and if humanity is becoming more heterogeneous, then the role of the propagandist as one who influences thought and feeling positively (toward the "truth") is going to take on more importance in the future than it has had in the past.

Byron B. Renz
Fort Collins, CO
February 15, 2009

REFERENCES

Ellul, Jacques. 1973. *Propaganda: The formation of men's attitudes,* Trans. Konrad Kellen and Jean Lerner. New York: Vintage Books.

Maurier, George du. 1894. *Trilby.* New York: Harper and Brothers.

McAuliffe, Kathleen. 2009. March. "Are We Still Evolving?" *Discover,* March: 51.

Chapter One

Media, Fear, and the Consolidation of State Power

Fear can have a stultifying effect on an individual. People cope with fear in a variety of ways to bring stability to the disequilibrium caused by the fear. But, fear can permeate a society, and, as with personal fear, societies seek coping mechanisms that strive to reduce the disequilibrium generated by fear.

Fear may take several different forms, but, essentially, it is a basic emotion. It is an unpleasant feeling of perceived risk or danger. Fear may also consist of an extreme dislike of some conditions or objects, such as fear of darkness or fear of being in narrow or enclosed spaces (claustrophobia).

Fear may generate behavior modification, substituting one behavior pattern with another. Behavior modification, however, does not always contain a fear element. Fearing objects or contexts can be learned. Fear conditioning, which depends on the emotional circuitry of the brain, is being studied in animals (Fear, 2005, 1). Fear has different degrees, including terror, fright, paranoia, horror, and a persecution complex. Fear can lead to social problems and irrational or dangerous actions; therefore, it is important to consider fear as a potential element in persuasive messages and, almost always, as a highly charged component of propaganda messages.

Because mass communication is nearly universal and nearly instantaneous today, fear elements can be transmitted to almost everyone on the globe through fear-imbued persuasive messages, particularly propaganda. Because fear can be generated quickly among large population groups, these population groups can react en masse and in force quickly. Without time to cool off and filter the message of fear through others, especially opinion leaders, and to allow some time for rational reflection, extreme, irrational action is increasingly likely as time is eliminated in the communication process.

As we know, message availability is nearly universal today; message availability is almost simultaneous in time with the occurrence of an event;

and portable communication technology allows for nearly universal and simultaneous interpersonal interaction in response to a received message. This
means that we are plugged in to a communication network that is with us
constantly—like the iPod and MP3 players plugged in to the ears of people
working out at a gym or wandering a college campus. By analogy, the suggestion is that we are ready recipients of almost any type of idea and ready to
be triggered by any emotion.

Terrorists use this direct access to the brain first by sending messages reflecting their terrorist acts to nearly everyone around the globe via the internet
and then seeking access to as many established news organizations as possible. Their actions—a beheading, a hostage taking, a suicide bombing—are
tailored perfectly to fit the event-oriented, time-constrained format of television news in particular and the event-oriented, space-constrained format of
print journalism.

The terrorist event contains the highest possible drama, is visually graphic,
and is constrained in time. The entire "story" of a beheading or a suicide bomb
explosion and its immediate aftermath or the seizing of a hostage at gunpoint
can be told, with a beginning, middle, and an end (to the event itself) within
the two-and-a-half minutes of a television news story. The terrorist event,
because of its savagery and complete contradiction of basic Western values
(and the values of nearly every other culture as well), is designed to trigger
extreme emotions—anger, disgust, rage, and fear. The extreme state of the
emotion is intended to short-circuit the usual lines of market-oriented persuasive appeals that incorporate fear as an element in a persuasive message. But,
this chapter discusses instant messaging as a modern phenomenon that can be
exploited by terrorists, as well as businesses and governments. Let's look at
some figures to see how extensive instant messaging has become.

TWENTY-FIRST CENTURY

Television and radio penetrate virtually every household (with multiple sets);
newspapers and magazines are available almost everywhere (even though
read less than previously); the portability of cell phones has facilitated interpersonal communication exponentially; three-quarters of all Americans have
access to the internet (with that figure reaching nearly 100 percent for teenag-
ers), and podcasting is capturing the fascination of millions of people around
the world (Levy, 2004). Visual images (still and moving), accompanied by
audio and text are exchanged widely and universally on YouTube and Face-
book. Cell phone cameras have multiplied the number of pictures taken and
the number of locations from which pictures can be taken.

Some of the specific figures are revealing. The three-quarters of Americans who have access to the internet spend "an average of twelve-and-a-half hours a week online . . . for those between 12 and 18, usage approaches 100 per cent (Levy, 2004). The internet is increasingly becoming the news source of choice for internet users. As Levy notes, "Internet users use the medium as their No. 1 source of news, despite worries about credibility" (2004, 14).

Opportunity for interpersonal interaction, where opinion can be expressed regarding newsworthy events, is increasing "with a new blogger [joining] the crowd every 40 seconds (Levy, 2002, 42). Some estimates peg the current number of blogs at 70 million worldwide, including deactivated sites and spam sites (Riley, 2005, 1). To demonstrate further the penetration of media communication channels, consider that in 2007, the average U.S. home received 118.6 channels (Nielsen, 2008, June 6, 1). As the number of channels available to a household increases, so does the number of channels tuned. In 2007, the average household tuned to 16, or 13%, of the 118.6 channels available for at least 10 minutes a week (Nielsen, 2008, June 6, 1). The average U.S. home has 2.5 people and 2.8 television sets. Digital cable exists in 31% of homes; 61% have wired cable hook-ups; 27% have satellite or specialized antenna systems (up from 19% in 2005); 82% of U.S. homes have more than one television set at home; and 87% of U.S. homes have a DVD player, with that technology overtaking VCRs, which are in 79% of households (Nielsen, 2008, June 6, 2). Given a choice of six media, one-third (33%) of children aged 8 to 17 say that the Web would be the medium that they would want if no others were possible (StatisticalResearch.com, 2005).

Nearly half a century ago, Marshall McLuhan observed:

> We have extended our central nervous system itself in a global embrace, abolishing both space and time as far as our planet is concerned. Rapidly, we approach the final phase of the extensions of man—the technological simulation of consciousness, when the creative process of knowing will be collectively and corporately extended to the whole of human society, much as we have already extended our senses and nerves by the various media. (McLuhan, 1964, 3-4)

Our consciousness today is so wrapped in media that our thoughts, emotions, attitudes, opinions, and values are being energized on a constant basis. The media surround our consciousness like a skein of thread. One of the emotions that resonate with troublesome and uncertain effect is fear, and fear can be used as a manipulative variable in state control of a society.

Political leaders are fully aware of their need to "interact" with their constituents through the media, and most leaders are also well aware of the effectiveness of the manipulation of the elements of fear as a mechanism of political control. That awareness is not new. At the Nuremberg trials, Hermann Göring observed the following:

> Naturally the common people do not want war: neither in Russia, nor England, nor, for that matter, in Germany. That is understood. But, after all, it is the leaders of the country who determine the policy and it is always a simple matter to drag the people along, whether it is a democracy, or a fascist dictatorship, or a parliament, or a communist dictatorship. Voice or no voice, the people can always be brought to the bidding of the leaders. That is easy. All you have to do is tell them they are being attacked, and denounce the peacemakers for lack of patriotism and exposing the country to danger. It works the same way in any country. (Hermann Wilhelm Göring, Nuremberg Trials, April 1946)

THE TERRORIST INTEREST IN
FEAR-INDUCING PERSUASIVE MESSAGES

The terrorist approach to fear generation involves a sudden, violent, media-oriented action (a hostage-taking, a beheading) with verbal threats designed to taunt the terrorist's target, affirm the increasing power and solidarity of the terrorist organization, and proclaim the superior cleverness of the terrorist group in comparison with the object of attack.

The combined effect of the alternating threat and attack is to elevate the general level of anxiety in a population and, eventually, erode its will and psychological determination to resist. This gradual erosion of popular will opens the door for government to strengthen its own political, military, and police base, which often includes imposing restrictions on civil liberties.

A classic example of a threat, at a time when al-Qaeda held several Americans as hostages, came with the January 19, 2006, announcement by al-Qaeda leader Osama bin Laden that new attacks were being prepared for the United States (Yahoo!News, AFP, 1/19/2006). The bin Laden comments, on audio tape, claimed that the increased security measures imposed by the United States since the September 11, 2001, attack on the country were having no effect on deterring attack on the American mainland (Keath, AP, 1/19/2006). The reason for the lack of attacks, the bin Laden tape asserted, was simply that preparation takes time and that that time was about up.

The persuasive intent in the message was multifaceted. First, bin Laden knew that, as an international "celebrity," his message would be carried around the world on all communication channels—as it was. Second, al-Qaeda knew that the re-emergence of bin Laden after more than a year without a confirmed message from him (the previous message was in December 2004), his image as a slippery eel, unable to be controlled by the

West, would increase his reputation as being cleverer than Western leaders. Third, the ability of al-Qaeda to operate almost at will in hostage taking and suicide bombing gave an aura of strength to the multi-fanged organization. Bin Laden added a note of irony by saying that the operations were being planned in Baghdad, which was under American occupation (Keath, 1/19/2006). The composite persuasive appeal in this message was that you are facing a powerful, dangerous, and clever opponent who can strike you at will and is shrewd enough to elude your best defensive efforts. Against such an opponent, the argument goes, one would have no option other than to yield, negotiate a truce (which is precisely what bin Laden offered), or renew one's ferocious counterattack.

The hypothesis of this chapter is that persuasive messages that bypass ideational development in a text and direct an argument to people's basic needs will result in a knee-jerk reaction that short-circuits the traditional bounds of argument in persuasion. Terrorists' actions contain an implicit argument. The terrorist's argument is unidimensional. It contains maximal emotion and no elaboration, which would consist of a train of thought suggesting a rational path to problem solution. That argument (conveyed by the terrorist's act) is directed repeatedly at the most primitive of human concerns—our survival and safety needs.

The significance of basic needs may be visualized by thinking about the pyramid that illustrates Maslow's (1954) hierarchy of needs. Man's most fundamental needs are those to which he is committed most deeply and would struggle hardest to protect. The base of Maslow's pyramid—the first level of needs that are fundamental to us—consists of our *physiological* needs—our requirements for survival, such as food, water, shelter, and sex. The second level in the pyramid consists of our *safety* needs (personal safety and security). This concerns the human desire to avoid physical and emotional harm and to feel protected and secure. These two levels represent our life-sustaining needs and, therefore, resonate most deeply in our minds.

The next three levels of needs in Maslow's pyramid move beyond the life-sustaining level into the level of self-realization. Maslow's third level consists of *belonging* needs (satisfaction through social interaction). This concerns people's desire to be accepted and acceptable members of society. The fourth need level consists of *esteem* needs (the need to sense our self-worth). This entails feeling good about oneself and with one's relationships with others. The fifth level—and the tip of the pyramid—consists of *self-actualization* needs (the need to realize our most cherished goals). Self-actualization refers to the human tendency to strive for ever-higher goals, to be the best person one can possibly be. The motivational power in these five pyramid levels decreases as one goes up the pyramid.

The lower down the pyramid a persuasive message is directed, the greater is the potential of that message to generate fear. In addition, a high-fear appeal directed at the lower two levels of Maslow's need pyramid results in less mental processing of idea and working through of the steps of the problem-solution process. There, the terrorist's persuasive message is not intended to result in rational solutions of problems; rather, it is intended to short-circuit rational thought processes and result in irrational behavior, such as blindly violent reaction or loss of confidence in one's ability to cope with the cause of the fear. The terrorist's persuasive message may also be intended to create a desire to seek compliant protection behind the shield of a powerful leader, or it may be intended to result in a collapse of the self in a pool of despair.

Let's look at two representative reactions of world leaders to the previously mentioned bin Laden announcement. President (George W.) Bush immediately rejected any suggestion that the United States government would negotiate with terrorists. More telling, however, was French President Jacques Chirac's reaction to the threat of terrorism on French soil. President Chirac said that France would be ready to use nuclear weapons against any state that carried out a terrorist attack against France. France's overall policy prohibits the use of nuclear weapons in a military conflict. But, the French president said that an exception might be made in the event of a terrorist attack (Pineau, Reuters, 1/19/2006). The seizing of American journalist Jill Carroll at about the same time as the release of the bin Laden tape delivered another emotionally charged message to the world. The seizing of hostages, with the subsequent release of controlled information about them, has become a terrorist "commercial" run on schedule to reinforce persistently the sponsor's message. More than 240 foreigners have been seized as hostages since the 2003 American-led invasion against Saddam Hussein in Iraq. Of those 240 captives, at least 39 have been killed (Yahoo!News, Reuters, 1/20/2006).

Several significant questions are raised at this point. Are appeals to fear effective persuasive devices? Are appeals to fear consistent in their effectiveness in the persuasive process? What types of fear appeals serve politicians' interests in consolidating their power?

THE GENERAL CHARACTER OF
FEAR-BASED PERSUASIVE MESSAGES

Marketers have generally accepted a curvilinear pattern for the use of fear appeals in advertising messages. The curvilinear pattern suggests that as levels of fear start to increase from the zero point on the inverted U, fear may have a motivating effect. The increase in fear to moderate levels tends to stimulate cognitive processes (thinking about) the object of fear. The thought process assumes the form of problem solving, and rational response strategies are formulated. As fear intensifies and reaches high levels, the rational problem-solving process starts to break down. Defense-motivated biased information processing begins, and irrational, self-protective strategies may be employed: (1) denial of the existence of the threat, (2) self-destructive responses, or (3) the use of blind power to reach out and destroy the threat. The person who walks blithely into the face of the threat, saying, "God will protect me," may illustrate the first condition.

The second condition may be illustrated by mass suicides, such as the incident at Jonestown, Guyana, November 18, 1978, during which the Reverend Jim Jones led more than 900 followers to their deaths by drinking a cyanide-laced grape punch. Cult members who refused to swallow the punch were shot (http://www.cnnj.com/US/9703/27/suicide.list/index.html, 12/29/2005).

The third condition may be illustrated by the systematic execution of hostages, such as the beheading on video in Iraq of American hostage Eugene Armstrong, September 20, 2004, who was killed by an al Zarqawi militant group, and American hostage Jack Hensley, September 22, 2004. Although fear may not have been the sole motivation for action in these instances, it contributed significantly to the resulting outcome—the use of power to put down the insurgents and increased resolve to locate and destroy as many al-Qaeda cells as possible. The interlacing of bitter irony with the fear-inspiring event was the fact that American hostages have often been suited in the same type of orange jumpsuits that the Americans have forced the al-Qaeda detainees to wear at Guantánamo Bay. It seems that when fear reaches a critical mass, systematic cognitive processing of information ceases to function, and the rational problem-solving process breaks down. Irrational responses supplant rational decision-making.

The relation between fear and relevant information levels is also significant. As fear rises in early and intermediate levels, it appears that information on the severity of the threat or the efficacy (effectiveness) of coping responses is relevant. Information is increasingly brought to bear on the source of concern. At the same time, irrelevant information is discarded (Meijnders, Midden, and Wilke, 2001).

Keller and Block support the concept that fear appeals at the two extremes are relatively ineffective in bringing about attitude change that would result in behavior consistent with some persuasive objective. The assumption here is that we are dealing with a rational process that includes fear appeal elements in a message, as well as idea that could lead to reasonable, thought-formulated problem solution. Keller and Block postulate that when low levels of fear in persuasive messages are ineffective, it is because there is insufficient elaboration of the harmful consequences of engaging in the destructive behavior. On the one hand, if a drinking and driving appeal that advocates appointment of a designated driver suggests that an automobile accident might result in stiffness of the joints and a few cuts, one would not be likely to elaborate on the solution, i.e., appoint a designated driver. On the other hand, when appeals arousing high levels of fear are ineffective, the reason is that too much elaboration on the harmful consequences interferes with processing of the desired change in behavior (Keller and Block, 1996). For example, if the persuasive appeal described the agony of severe mutilation in gory detail, one might engage in defensive denial of the message (The person might say, "That doesn't apply to me."), or one might deny the importance of the message ("Things other than drinking cause traffic accidents, too.") In both cases, elaboration on the steps recommended in the solution is minimal. Remember that the terrorist's message, so far, has been constructed of high-fear, minimal-thought content.

Defensive Strategies to High Fear-Appeal Messages

Several studies have indicated that high fear arousal is often countered by defensive maneuvers on the part of the message receivers. The defensive techniques include (1) avoiding the message, (2) minimizing the severity of the threat, (3) selectively attending to the message, (4) discounting the threat, and (5) denying the personal relevance of the threat (Eagly and Chaiken, 1993; Rogers 1983). One would be wise to consider these defensive maneuvers when considering the strategy behind the terrorist's persuasive message.

The nature of fear itself describes the way that fear ultimately influences behavior (focused action that is responsive to a sequence of events—terrorist acts, in this instance). Henthorne, LaTour, Rotfeld, and others have identified "tension" and "energy" as elements of the emotional arousal that we define as fear. Tension is characterized by high activation. Energy arousal is characterized by "tenseness" and "jittery" feelings. Energy arousal is a psycho-physiological response that is characterized by feelings of "pep" or energy. Subsequent findings supported a premise that if tension levels do not cross a hypothetical threshold, they will generate energy arousal and result in positive feelings toward the ad stimulus. However, if the tension levels cross the "hypothetical threshold" (becoming very strong), they will "drive down" energy arousal and will result in negative feelings toward the ad stimulus (LaTour and Rotfeld, 1997).

These conclusions seem to be essentially in agreement with Keller and Block's suggestion that problem elaboration is easier to achieve with low-fear appeals than with high-fear appeals. As the emotion of fear is elevated to high levels, the highly concentrated feeling makes it difficult to think rationally about a solution to the problem and to ponder in a moderate time frame the sequence of steps required to see the solution through to its conclusion. High-tension levels require time compression. Quick, powerful, violent, blind action is needed to achieve immediate tension reduction. Therefore, as Keller and Block suggest, high-fear appeals should be more persuasive than low-fear appeals if problem elaboration is discouraged in the message. Problem elaboration refers to a situation in which people may consider systematic, ideationally based steps to solve a problem. An effort to blend the low-emotion appeal, which allows for rational sequences of thought, with the high-emotion appeal, which short-circuits rational lines of thought, becomes contradictory. Such a contradiction would seem to be especially true if the fear messages related to the most basic of human interests, the maintenance of life itself and personal safety and security, the lower two levels of Maslow's hierarchy of needs.

Theories of Anxiety

Several theories of anxiety have been set forth. Each contributes something to our understanding of the way that anxiety relates to physiological arousal and cognition, and each contributes something to our understanding of the way that terrorists' efforts rely on a pattern of irrational persuasion. Feedback theory says that heightened arousal of the sympathetic nervous system has a causal role in determining emotional experience. James-Lange (1898) propounded the best-known theory that suggests that emotional arousal depends on prior physiological arousal. The essence of that theory is that "we feel sorry because we cry, angry because we strike, afraid because we tremble, and not that we cry, strike, or tremble because we are sorry, angry, fearful, as the case may be" (cited in Eysenck, 28).

The more popular theory these days that describes the causation of emotion is based on cognitive appraisal of anxiety-producing situations. For example, Schachter and Singer (1962) and Schachter (1964) developed a theory of emotion in which they said that emotional experience depends on three factors. First, a given situation must be interpreted as being an emotional one. Second, physiological arousal must occur. Third, the emotional situation must be perceived as being the cause of the physiological arousal (Schachter and Singer, 1962, and Schachter, 1964). With any of these three factors missing, little or no emotion will be experienced. Terrorist persuasive communications, of course, strike all three chords with force.

Appraisal Theory

Emotion is caused by a cognitive evaluation of some situation or event, according to appraisal theorists. Appraisal theorists say that emotions are rarely a direct reaction to some stimulus. Instead, it is the relevance of the emotional impact to the individual's personal concerns that gives the object emotional impact (Parkinson, 1994). The keying of terrorist persuasive messages to the lowest two levels of Maslow's hierarchy of needs zeros in directly on the fundamental concern about an individual's safety and security.

Lazarus (1966, 1982, 1991) expanded upon the cognitive appraisal process and suggested that the forms of appraisal can be subdivided into three parts. The first of these parts is primary appraisal. Here, the situation is assessed as being positive, stressful, or irrelevant to one's personal well-being. The second cognitive occurrence involves a secondary appraisal. At this stage, the person considers and evaluates the resources at his disposal, which would allow him to cope with the situation. The third step involves reappraisal. The primary and secondary appraisals are evaluated and modified if necessary. A terrorist message, announcing mayhem, certainly encourages stress. Because the terrorist message is aimed at a country, its political system, its economic system, and its culture, the widespread distribution of its emotional appeal is virtually universal and impactful. The secondary appraisal step is particularly significant for government officials of the defending Western democracies. The individual recoils at this threat but feels himself personally powerless to defend himself against the hooded, automatic weapon-wielding band of terrorists. This personal sense of helplessness encourages the individual to draw himself in behind the protective shield of his government resources, the military and the police. One must support the power that provides the protective shield. The only logical conclusion is to support the political party that controls the government at a particular time. With a direct, unidimensional message, such as those that the terrorists send, the reappraisal process seldom occurs. There is no logical need for it.

Anxiety in Long-Term Memory

The experience of anxiety in relation to long-term memory is relevant when considering the effects of terrorist events on the creation of anxiety. One source of information for the experience of anxiety consists of cognitions relating to information stored in long-term memory. These cognitions usually take the form of worries. Worries are important cognitions with respect to the emotion of anxiety. It isn't so much the number of worries contained in long-term memory; rather, it is the tendency to attend selectively to the information that makes up the worry in conjunction with its interpretation (Eysenck 1997).

Eysenck's (1997) four-factor theory of anxiety sheds some light on the long-term effects of anxiety. Anxiety is a particularly significant emotion as it relates to the sustained effect of continued terrorist fear messages. The first of the four assumptions of this theory is that four sources of information determine the level of experienced anxiety: (1) cognitive appraisal of the situation; (2) perceived level of behavioral anxiety; (3) perceived level of physiological anxiety; and (4) negative cognitions from long-term memory. With the terrorist message, we evaluate the terrorist situation mutually and develop a mental concept of its scope and depth.

The second assumption in the four-factor theory is that the effects of these four sources of information on experienced anxiety depend on attentional and interpretive biases normally operating below conscious levels. The anxiety regarding the terrorist message depends on the frequency with which the mind drifts to thoughts about the terrorist situation and the pool of opinion that colors the internal response to the thought.

The third assumption of the four-factor theory of anxiety is that one's cognitive biases become greater as state anxiety increases. State anxiety, as opposed to trait anxiety, is dependent upon the perception of an external situation rather than one's psychological characteristics and is "characterized by subjective, consciously perceived feelings of tension and apprehension, and heightened autonomic nervous system activity" (Spielberger, Gorsuch & Lushene, 1970, 3).

The fourth assumption of the four-factor theory is that schemas or organized packets of knowledge stored in long-term memory affect the functioning of the cognitive biases. In short, negative information in long-term memory can increase anxiety. The most intense emotional feeling associated with worry is anxiety, followed by feelings related to anxiety, such as tension, apprehension, and nervousness (Eysenck 1997).

Repression of Fear

It is useful to know, too, as one considers fear and the response to fear texts in messages that some people tend to repress their response to fear stimuli by saying that they are less fearful than they actually are. Therefore, gathering self-reports of people's perceptions of the level of fear actually experienced may underestimate the actual level of fear being experienced. For example, Sparks, Pellechia, and Irvine (1999) identify certain persons as "repressive copers." These are persons who tend to cope with stressful stimuli by "repressing the expression of negative affect [and who] may show up in mass communication studies as individuals who report low levels of fear to frightening stimuli. In such cases, the low levels of self-reported fear may be more indicative of the tendency to repress emotion than anything else" (Sparks, Pellechia, and Irvine, 1999, 177).

Some people who are exposed to frightening mass media repress their negative emotional reactions, with the result that their self-reports indicate low levels of emotional reaction even though their body physiology indicates the exact opposite. The Sparks et al. study suggests the possibility that repressive copers are relatively aware of their negative emotional reaction and that repressive copers simply deny that they are frightened when asked to express it in a self-report. The authors conclude that if negative emotion is mainly conscious, then persons who are denying their emotion may experience negative consequences from repeated media exposure, such as nightmares or haunting images. If negative emotion is unconscious, then no outward manifestation of psychological stress would be evident. The conclusions of this study may suggest a cumulative negative affect regarding news reports of terrorist activities. If the results of this study are distributable to reactions to truncated, high-fear appeal terrorist messages, it would be reasonable to conclude that we may not be seeing the full negative consequences of terrorist persuasive messages.

Protection Motivation Theory

Protection motivation theory adds a significant dimension to our discussion of fear arousal and problem solution. This theory is concerned with the ways that people process threats and the ways that people determine responses that would allow them to cope with the danger posed by those threats. Protection motivation theory suggests that the persuader add coping response information to fear appeals. Such information would route coping behaviors into appropriate channels. In essence, a threat-oriented appeal that is designed to generate fear alone is seen as less effective than an appeal that also contains information that suggests an appropriate coping response (Tanner, Day, and Crask, 1989). In a terrorist message, coping response information is implied and is part of the design of the terrorist's persuasive message.

Bandura (1977), in a work on expectancy of self-efficacy, suggests that having effective coping defenses prohibits fear arousal. Self-efficacy expectancy is the perception of one's ability to perform a particular behavior. The emotion (fear, in this case) and cognition (the assessment of the danger) interact in an effort to find a successful coping behavior. Fear is not aroused if the coping behaviors of the person are sufficient to respond adequately to the problem. Fear is aroused if the repertory of behaviors does not include coping responses perceived to be adequate to deal with the threat. The purpose of fear, at this point, is to lead the person to look for a more effective behavior. With a threat the size of international terrorism, the individual has little choice other than to support the institutions of society that may offer broad-based protection—the police, the military, and information-gathering agencies under the direction of the federal government.

Protection motivation theory is more concerned with behavior than with fear per se. It is concerned with the danger-control process. Originally, the protection motivation model included three separate cognitive processes: (1) the appraised severity of the threat, (2) the expectancy of exposure, i.e., the probability of its occurrence, and (3) one's belief in the efficacy of a coping response. Because fear is an emotion, it played no part in the cognitive process (Tanner, Day, and Crask, 1989).

Maddux and Rogers (1983) expanded meaningfully on protection motivation theory. Their study concluded that knowledge of the coping response did not necessarily mean that the person would adopt that response. For a response to be adopted, a person must also believe in his ability to perform that behavior. Four variables were manipulated: (1) the severity of the threat, (2) the probability of occurrence of the threat, (3) the coping response efficacy, and (4) self-efficacy. The hypothesis was that a person who believes that he is capable of performing an effective coping behavior in response to a serious threat that is highly probable would adopt the coping response. Although the study results were not completely consistent with expectations, the authors concluded that "maladaptive coping responses may be an unintended result of fear appeal "communication. But frightening the audience is not the objective—promoting responsible behavior is" (Tanner, Day, and Crask, 1989, 275). In essence, protection motivation theory suggests that the focus of a persuasive message should not be on the fear component of the message; rather, the focus of the message should be on the danger inherent in a situation, coupled with an effective coping response and the ability of the audience to implement that coping response.

Collective Message from the Studies of Fear

So, what do the collective psychological studies of fear tell us? They suggest that a fear component may function as a legitimate element in the construction of a persuasive message. The curvilinear pattern suggests that fear and cognitive components may interact at various intensity levels to provide a motivation to act (from the fear component) and to provide a direction toward problem solution (from the cognitive component). Terrorists, of course, modify that pattern to achieve irrational ends. When fear reaches high levels, it disrupts the process of rational thought.

Psychological studies of fear also tell us that the nature of the impact of the fear element is dependent upon whether we have information that suggests paths to the solution of the problem. Minimizing problem-solving information creates a no-exit anxiety that destabilizes rational thought processes and leads to irrational reactions. Psychological studies also warn us that we may not always have a clear understanding of the magnitude of fear, because high fear arousal often results in defensive maneuvers that obscure the size and nature of the fear. If we can't know it accurately, we will be less successful in predicting its result.

The tension and energy aroused by fear should normally lead to rational action intended to solve the problem. With opaque or only translucent paths to problem solution, the energy generated from fear may implode into a nebulous worry and its stultifying corollary, anxiety. Again, the nature of the terrorist's persuasive message construct is to immobilize the enemy, not to invite positive problem solution.

The terrorist's persuasive message meets all of the requirements of cognitive appraisal of anxiety-producing situations: (1) interpreting a situation as emotional, (2) experiencing physiological arousal, and (3) associating the emotional situation with the arousal. The four-factor theory of anxiety adds the significant dimension of knowledge packets stored in long-term memory. These packets affect cognitive biases. Negative information in long-term memory feeds anxiety. These conclusions suggest a powerful potential of negative fear appeals to affect the collective psyche of an entire society. Once we understand the problem, we can look for rational problem solutions.

Because fear is an emotion, it is inherently temporal and differs from despair in that it requires that one have the ability to envisage alternatives to a future dominated by terrorists and their acts of brutality. Skidmore (2003) notes that Burmese people try not to express fear in response to the emotional climate created in their authoritarian state. She notes that fear is experienced as a distortion and disorientation of perspective. Fear creates a surreal dimension to everyday life that "emphasizes negative aspects to such a large extent that thoughts involving the future are flattened and silenced" (Skidmore, 2003, 10). The Burmese military maintains fear and an atmosphere of emergency in two ways. The first is by creating a fear of the Other. This could be fear of a neocolonial presence, a foreigner, an internal traitor, or simply a change from the status quo. The Burmese people are encouraged to be vigilant in the face of threats posed by the Other.

The second strategy used by the Burmese military regime is to point out that the safe path for the Union of Myanmar is progress, with progress being defined by the military. Skidmore says that to generate fear, the military confuses, distorts, and controls time. The objective is to stop the Burmese people from imagining a future other than one that requires their incorporation into a totalitarian state. Intentionally generated fear and terror facilitate control of the population through disorientation. In the case of Myanmar, according to Skidmore, the government uses both external and internal threats to generate fear-inducing messages. In the United States, the government capitalizes on external threats—the potential attack by terrorists—and spins that threat into fear-generating messages.

By contrast, acts of non-state terrorism are designed to influence a society in a more indirect manner than the state-generated fear in Myanmar described by Skidmore. Picard (1993) says that terrorist acts are designed to influence society and to create societal conditions in which the behavior of social institutions can be changed, in which power distribution among institutions can be changed, or in which power distribution between institutions and the populace can be changed. These acts of violence are designed to produce effects, to shape attitudes, and to influence behavior. Therefore, these acts may be considered a form of persuasive communication.

Nature of the Terrorist Persuasive Act

Our discussion of fear-generating messages so far has typically included a verbal and visual text, with a logical appeal incorporated in the text. This is the typical laboratory condition created for many empirical studies of the use of fear in persuasive messages. Terrorist acts have a different dimension. A terrorist act is usually an emotionally charged visual event that is diametrically opposed to the fundamental values of a society—a proscription against murder, for example. The stunning blow delivered by the media message reporting an event is designed not only to generate fear, but also to create a powerful, negatively charged opinion toward the terrorists. The primary purpose of that opinion, although obscured by the act itself, is designed to create government reaction that will harm the public and create a restlessness that will stir the government into drastic reactions that will change the relationship between the citizens and the state. As Picard notes, "history has shown that the crystallization of opinion has generally resulted in support for government efforts to halt terrorism" (Picard, 1993, 43).

A terrorist act is a form of propaganda, but terrorist acts are not designed to persuade the receivers of the media messages to support the cause of the terrorist. Rather, Picard states that, "As a form of propaganda . . . terrorism is most like psychological warfare because it attempts to demoralize; to induce fear, anxiety, and lack of confidence in leadership; and to lead to instability in society that terrorists can further exploit for their purposes" (Picard, 1993, 46). Picard says that terrorists rely upon the concept of the propaganda of the deed. The messages normally conveyed in this type of propaganda are that the non-state terrorists are effective, that there is reason to fear the terrorists, that people are unhappy with the status quo, and that authorities are not fully in control (Picard, 1993).

THE TERRORIST ACT AS A SOURCE OF NEWS

The terrorist act is a very effective vehicle for generating news coverage, because the event fits neatly into the Western news frame. It can be reported on briefly; it is dramatic; and it fits the we-they duality of a conflict between opponents. This telling of a story within rigid time or space constraints results in a distortion of the scope and nature of terrorism, but such distortion often occurs because media coverage is reactive rather than anticipatory.

Western media rely on an event-oriented, rather than idea-oriented, concept of journalism. Individuals or groups wanting access to the media have learned to create what Daniel J. Boorstin described as "pseudo-events." These are contrived events designed to obtain media coverage, with the objective of gaining attention (Boorstin, 1961).

The expectation that it is events that constitute news keeps reporters from exploring trends in social problems and putting problems and events in some context. "As a result," Picard says, "audiences, including authorities, are forced to confront terrorism at the micro rather than the macro level. This makes it possible for authorities to argue that society must deal with the manifestations of social problems—that is, the acts of terrorism and their effects—rather than the social problems themselves" (Picard, 1993, 112).

The most important sources for foreign news in the United States are the agencies of the federal government, in particular the White House, the State Department, and the Pentagon. These agencies manage the flow of news about foreign countries that arises from an international crisis. Information is sometimes withheld—as may be the case with civil rights violations—or released selectively to a small group of "authorities," which, in turn, release the information through journalistic interviews. The selective release of information is common in response to reports of terrorism. The public gets the information from television or the newspapers from authorities whose most up-to-date information has come from the government (see Lang and Lang, 2000). The corresponding news story is developed as a crisis—often involving opposing antagonists—and generates fear, which the government attempts to allay through demonstrating its strength and competence. Lang and Lang state, "Television news, even more than newspapers, has generally been driven by crisis, conflicts, and disaster, a pattern also manifest in news that comes from abroad" (Lang and Lang, 2000, 300). In recent years, terrorism should be added to the list. Also, in recent years, the forces just cited driving news may be applied to the BBC World News and the international edition of Deutsche Welle (German broadcasting).

Altheide (1997) suggests that the problem frame used by the media to discuss issues, both in news and entertainment formats, is a major factor in producing societal fear. Much media programming deals with issues, but the issues are usually cast as "problems." A "problem" fits more neatly in the narrative storytelling structure of both news and entertainment programming than does the examination of an issue in the more loosely structured discussion-resolution format. Altheide says, "The problem frame promotes a discourse of fear that may be defined as the pervasive communication, symbolic awareness and expectation that danger and risk are a central feature of the effective environment" (Altheide, 648).

It should be noted that the creation of fear is subject to social influence. Society teaches people to worry about subjects such as money, status, sin and salvation, personal relationships, health, crime, and obesity (Altheide, 1997). Even though the target of fear is socially constructed, it is perceived as "real" and, therefore, has consequences. Social interaction and communication, including mass communication, provide the foundation for fear. And, the fear that is of primary concern to the sociologist concerns an anxiety held in common in a community, not an individual fear (see Altheide, 1997). Such is the case with the terrorist message.

The creation of fear needs to be associated with an enemy, and an enemy can be defined most concretely by creating a dichotomous image. The dichotomous image is created verbally by use of words such as "we" versus "they." Coloring in of the negative image occurs through reference to "evil" (or the "evil empire"), "demons," or, euphemistically, "those people." A nation needs "enemies" (see Merskin, 2004). A government uses the idea of a common enemy as a method of social control, a method of reinforcing the political, economic, and cultural values of the nation and as a mechanism for reinforcing those beliefs (see Keen, 1986; Spillman and Spillman, 1997). A common enemy can distract attention from other issues that a government might want to obscure. In addition, a common enemy allows for the creation of survival strategies that are grounded in the value and belief system of a nation. The United States has taken several major steps to consolidate information-gathering authority, police power, and broad-based physical security efforts since 9/11.

In considering fear arousal in relation to argument construction, it is worth noting that problem elaboration is influenced by self-reference. Reference to the self may include a variety of types of knowledge. These may include one's physical appearance, one's past experiences, one's behavioral patterns, one's feelings toward one's attitudes, and one's relationship with others (Janis and Feshbach, 1953). Therefore, events encoded with respect to the self allow for more extensive elaboration than events encoded in relation to others (Bower and Gilligan, 1979; Burnkrant and Unnava, 1995). Receivers of persuasive messages, based on fear appeals, engage in greater elaboration on a problem when a situation allows them to imagine themselves suffering the consequences of noncompliance with the persuasive message. The application of this concept in relation to the terrorist message may be seen in the image of a helpless hostage, kneeling fearfully in front of a group of hooded, heavily armed men. Such an image allows easy vicarious identification with the victim. The viewer shudders to think of himself in place of the victim. Yet, even the visual elaboration occurring through the motion picture of the mind leads to a short-circuited dead end of emotion. As noted, the nature of the terrorist's persuasive message discourages rational problem-solving.

Essentially, the Keller-Block argument is that a low-fear appeal should be more persuasive than a high-fear appeal when the message encourages problem elaboration (following a particular course of action to resolve a problem). In other words, a low-fear appeal should generate more problem and solution thoughts when the message suggests a solution to the problem, especially where self-reference and imagery processing occur. A high-fear appeal, on the other hand, should be more persuasive than a low-fear appeal if problem elaboration is discouraged in the message, i.e., there is not a satisfactory path for personal solution to the problem. Problem elaboration, in this context, refers to ideational elements that may be used to achieve rational solutions to problems. The term *elaboration* may also be used to refer to the motion-picture-of-the-self in the mind as the self identifies vicariously with the image of someone on a screen, such as a hostage being beheaded. A high-fear message still results, however, in a rational problem-solution dead end.

Individual responses to fear and the adoption of appropriate coping strategies may be extended to societies at large. A major instigator of societal concern today is terrorism. Its threats and the ramifications of those threats are a source of repeated surges of societal fear. Most definitions of political terrorism imply that the creation of fear is an intention of the terrorist. Corsi (1981) suggests that different levels of fear are related to different types of terrorism and styles of communication that are associated with each type of terrorism. Essentially, Corsi examines terrorist attacks against individuals (hostage taking) and attacks against property (a night club or the World Trade Center).

Where hostages are taken and their lives threatened, fear is focused on the immediate hostages. Their lives are held in the balance while terrorists and authorities bargain. In attacks on property, terrorists intend to create a more general societal fear. The distributive interpretation of that message is that "certain types of targets are intrinsically unsafe or that any public place might be subject to terrorist attack" (Corsi, 51-52).

Regardless of whether the focus is immediate or general, fear may arise in a population at large. Fear generated in a hostage crisis situation would likely arise as a result of an audience member's vicarious identification with the victim. Such a conclusion is consistent with the Bower and Gilligan (1979) observation that greater elaboration on a problem occurs when a situation allows the receivers of a persuasive message to visualize themselves suffering as a result of failure to comply with the directive in the message. Nevertheless, the culmination of the visual elaboration is a dead end of emotion—fear. Fear generated from an attack or a threatened attack on property would likely result in a blunter hammer blow to the message recipient. The effect would be the equivalent of an earth tremor. There is no safe place to go.

Whether the threat in the terrorist's message is individually focused or societally focused, the creation of repressive political regimes on the part of nations subject to terrorist attack may be the precise goal of the terrorists (Marighella, 1971a, 1971b).

Corsi says,

By imparting general fear, [property attacks] can create the impression that a society's law enforcement and protection mechanisms are ineffective. At the same time, the infringement resulting from an aggressive law enforcement response may sufficiently limit civil liberties to generate a substantial level of dissatisfaction. Meanwhile, terrorists are ready to act as a vanguard, channeling this dissatisfaction into an anti-regime revolution. (Corsi, 52)

Nevertheless, fear is an emotion that must rise and fall over time. Any arousal of tension constitutes a disequilibrium that must return to a state of equilibrium. Therefore, the result of the consistent arousal of emotion related to the same subject—terrorism, in this case—is an attitude shift against the person, institution, or idea that is the impetus of the fear. The new attitude, distributed across a societal base, provides an appetite for persuasive political messages that provide problem solutions that feed the appetite of the political electorate. These messages come to us through political speeches and news conferences by governmental leaders and through the content of media messages generated by public relations organizations serving governmental interests.

Repeated reports of terrorist events generate fear arousals, which, repeatedly and over time, create an attitudinal foundation that is conducive to political appeals to increase national security and to decrease the threat of security breaches by destroying the source of the attacks from abroad. The source of power to protect national security resides in the military, the police, and the legislature, which has the authority to pass more or less stringent laws regarding the levels of freedom of the citizenry. The entrenched political party is the only organization that can promise direct action that will respond to the attitudinal predisposition of the electorate and that will reduce the incidence of events that periodically arouse fear. The executive branch can employ military and police powers; the legislature can approve legislation intended to increase the safety of the citizenry (which often includes restrictions of citizen freedoms). We are advised to be eternally vigilant. And, yet, a society would be well advised to keep in mind the words of Nietzsche, when he said, "Simply by being compelled to keep constantly on his guard, a man may grow so weak as to be unable any longer to defend himself" (Nietzsche, *Ecce Homo*, 1888).

So far, this chapter has examined the nature and use of fear in persuasive messages and the role of media in disseminating messages with a fear component. This author believes that two other factors should be considered in a discussion of the kind of fear generated by terrorism and its consequences for society. It seems intuitive to assume that the farther down the hierarchy of human concerns a fear message is keyed, the more powerful would be the reaction. As mentioned previously, this idea might be visualized through Maslow's hierarchy of needs. Physiological needs are most important and are the base of the triangle. Safety needs rank second in importance, followed by social needs, esteem needs, and, finally, self-actualization needs. It stands to reason that the farther down the hierarchy of need significance one goes to find a fertile field for a powerful persuasive message based on fear, the greater potential resides in that message to strengthen or alter the belief system of a population to achieve significant behavior change. In other words, when fear touches deep within the hierarchy of needs, more exaggerated consequences can be expected from the persuasive message. Such consequences—based on highly charged messages—may range from one polar opposite, such as denial, to the other polar opposite, such as murder or suicide. Messages keyed to the lower levels of the hierarchical triangle, with moderate levels of appeals to fear would more likely result in more moderate, controlled responses, responses that would allow for message elaboration and logical consideration in behavior modification.

THE SOCIAL CONSTRUCTION OF REALITY

Sociology tells us that an individual is, in varying degrees, molded by his social relations. Our sense of self is shaped by the language we use, the type of education to which we are exposed, and the norms and values that we learn at home, among our peers, as part of teams, in school, at work, at church, and within our social groups. The thinking, acting, reacting self is shaped largely through our relations with other people. These relations gradually shape our sense of identity and individuality (see Littlejohn, 2002; Croteau and Hoynes, 2003). The social construction of reality is not an argument per se, of course, but, like the syllogistic argument, it frames the reality that we experience. It frames the way in which we receive the terrorist's message, the way that we perceive that message, and the way that we respond to that message.

As Littlejohn (2002) notes, "virtually any aspect of human experience can be viewed from the perspective of how it is made and used in the social construction of reality" (165). The resources for the social construction of reality include ideas, values, stories, symbols, meanings, institutions, and whatever else may be used to build a reality. These collected elements contribute to the perceptions that we hold of the world around us. Although perceptions aren't the total sum of reality, we act on our perceptions, thus making them a real part of existence. The resources for the social construction are shared with other people. Therefore, the values that become associated with our images and ideas are constructed jointly through interaction in society.

Littlejohn (2002) says that when a person looks at an object that was designed by people who interacted to bring that design into fruition, one is using communication in the construction of that reality. Littlejohn cites, as an example, "architecture [which] is a form of expression in which designers, builders, and users make a certain social world. The cultures of the world differ substantially in how they express their values and beliefs through the kinds of buildings and homes they make" (165).

Communication, as persuasion used in terrorist messages, and the way that those images are constructed to create an image of the enemy and to suggest the relation of the enemy to one's own society are the concepts that will be treated next in chapter 2 and chapter 3. This, then, becomes the architecture of persuasion as it is used in propaganda.

REFERENCES

Altheide, David L. 1997. The news media, the problem frame, and the production of fear. *The Sociological Quarterly*, 38, 4, 647-668.

Bandura, Albert. 1977. Self-efficacy: Toward a unifying theory off behavioral change. *Psychological Review*, 84, 191-215.

Borstin, Daniel. J. 1961. *The image: A guide to pseudo-events in America*. New York: Harper Colophon Books.

Bower, Gordon H, and Stephen G. Gilligan. 1979. Remembering information related to one's self. *Journal of Research in Personality*, 13, 420-432.

Burnkrant, Robert E., and H. Rao Unnava. 1995. Effects of self-referencing on persuasion. *Journal of Consumer Research*, 22 (June), 17-26.

Corsi, Jerome R. 1981. Terrorism as a desperate game: Fear, bargaining, and communication in the terrorist event. *The Journal of Conflict Resolution*, March, 25, 1, 47-48.

Croteau, David, and William Hoynes. 2003. *Media society: Industries, images, and audience,* 3rd ed. Thousand Oaks, CA: Pine Forge Press.

Eagly, Alice H, and Shelly Chaiken. 1993. *The psychology of attitude.* Orlando, FL: Harcourt Brace Jovanovich.

Eysenck, Michael. W. 1997. *Anxiety and cognition: A unified theory.* East Sussex, UK: Psychology Press Publishers.

Fear. 2005. *Absolute Astronomy*, June 14:1-2. Accessed January 6, 2007, from http://www.absoluteastronomy.com/encyclopedia/f/fe/fear.htm

Göring, Hermann W. April 18, 1946. Nuremberg trials. Interview with U.S. Army Captain Gustave Gilbert. In G. M. Gilbert *Nuremberg diary,* 1947, New York: Farrar Straus: 268-279.

Halpern, Dick. 2005. More kids say internet is the medium they can't live without, April 15. Accessed December 29, 2005, from Statistical Research.com

Janis, Irving L, and Seymour Feshbach. 1953. Effects of fear-arousing communications. *Journal of Abnormal and Social Psychology*, 48, 78-92.

Keath, Lee. 2006. Yahoo!News. Bin Laden warns of attacks, offers truce, January 19. AP. Accessed January 19, 2006, from http://news.yahoo.com/s/ap/20060119

Keen, Sam. 1986. Faces of the enemy: Reflections of the hostile imagination. San Francisco: Harper & Row.

Keller, Punam A, and Lauren G. Block. 1996. Increasing the persuasiveness of fear appeals: The effects of arousal and elaboration. *The Journal of Consumer Research*, March, 22,4, 448-459.

Lang, Kurt, and Gladys E. Lang. 2000. How Americans view the world: Media images and public knowledge. In *Media power, professionals and policies,* ed. Howard Tumber, 295-313. New York: Routledge.

LaTour, Michael S, and Herbert J. Rotfeld. 1997. There are threats and (maybe) fear-caused arousal: Theory and confusions of appeals to fear and fear arousal itself, *Journal of Advertising,* Fall. *26, 3,* 46-59.

Lazarus, Richard S. 1966. *Psychological stress and the coping process.* New York: McGraw-Hill.

——. 1982. Thoughts on the relations between emotion and cognition. *American Psychologist*, 37, 1019-1024.

——. 1991. *Emotion and adaptation.* Oxford: Oxford University Press

Levy, Steven. 2002. Living in the blog-osphere. *Newsweek,* August 26, *140, 9,* 42.

——. 2004. No net? We'd rather go without food. *Newsweek,* October 11, *144, 15,*14. See also SRI (StatisticalResearch.com [a market research survey company, Westfield, NJ]).

Littlejohn, Stephen W. 2002. *Theories of human communication* (7th ed.). Belmont, CA: Wadsworth.

Maddux, James E. and Robert W. Rogers. 1983. Protection motivation and self-efficacy: A revised theory of fear appeals and attitude change. *Journal of Experimental Social Psychology*, September, *19*, 469-479.

Marighella, Carlos. 1971a. *For the liberation of Brazil*. Trans. John Butt and Rosemary Sheed. New York: Viking.

———. 1971b. Minimanual of the urban guerilla. In Robert Moss, *Urban guerilla warfare:* 20-42. London: International Institute for Strategic Studies.

Maslow, Abraham H. 1954. *Motivation and personality* (2nd ed.). New York: Harper and Row.

Meijnders, Anneloes L., Cees J. H. Midden, and Henk A.M. Wilke. 2001. Communication about environmental risks and risk-reducing behavior: The impact of fear on information processing. *Journal of Applied Social Psychology*, 31, 4, 754-777.

Merskin, Debra. 2004. The construction of Arabs as enemies: Post-September 11 discourse of George W. Bush. *Mass Communication and society*, 7, 2, 157-175.

McLuhan, Marshall. 1964. *Understanding media: The extensions of man*. New York: McGraw-Hill Book Company, 3-4.

Nielsen Media Research. 2004. In *The World Almanac and Book of Facts*, March 2005. New York: World Almanac Books, 311.

Nielsen—Press Release. 2008. NAverage U.S. home now receives a record 118.6 TV channels, June 6. Accessed January 26, 2009, from http://www.nielsen.com/media/2008/pr_080606.html.

Nietzsche, Friedrich W. 1888. *Ecce homo: How one becomes what one is*. Trans. Anthony M. Ludovici. Mineola, NY: Dover Publications (2004), 1911 Document. Book Libraries Worldwide, 12 (WorldCat).

Parkinson, Brian. 1994. Emotion. In *Companion encyclopaedia of psychology (Vol. 2)*. Ed. Andrew M. Colman. London: Routledge.

Picard, Robert G. 1993. *Media portrayals of terrorism: Functions and meaning of news coverage*. Ames, IA: Iowa State University Press.

Pineau, Elizabeth. 2006. Yahoo!News. France would use nuclear weapons against Terrorism, January 19. Accessed January 19, 2006, from http://news.yahoo.com/s/nm/20060119.

Riley, Duncan. 2005. Blog count for July: 70 million blogs. *The Blog Herald*, July 19:1. Accessed January 26, 2009, from http://www.blogherald.com/2005/07/19/blog-count-for-july-70 million-blogs/-61k.

Rogers, Ronald W. 1983. Cognitive and physiological processes in fear appeals and Attitude change: A revised theory of protection motivation. In John T. Cacioppo and Richard E. Petty, eds. *Social psychophysiology: A sourcebook*. New York: Guilford, 153-176.

Schachter, Stanley and Jerome E. Singer, 1962. Cognitive, social, and physiological determinants of emotional state. *Psychological Review, 69*, 379-399.

Schachter, Stanley. 1964. The interaction of cognitive and physiological determinants of emotional state. In Leon Festinger, ed, *Advances in experimental social psychology (Vol. 2)*. London: Routledge.

Schwartz, Tony. 1973. *The responsive chord*. Garden City, NY: Anchor Press/ Doubleday, 151.

Skidmore, Monique. 2003. Darker than midnight: Fear, vulnerability, and terror making in urban Burma (Myanmar). *American Ethnologist, 30, 1*, 5-21.

Sparks, Glenn G., Marianne Pellechia, and Chris Irvine. 1999. The repressive coping style and fright reactions to mass media. *Communication Research*, 26, 2 (April) 176-192.

Spielberger, Charles D., Richard L. Gorsuch, and Robert E. Lushene. 1970. The State Inventory (STAI) test manual. Palo Alto, CA: Consulting Psychologists Press.

Spillman, Kurt R., and Kati Spillman. 1997. Some sociobiological and psychological aspects of "Images of the Enemy." In Ragnhild Fisbig von Has and Ursula Lehmkuhl, eds. *Enemy images in American history*, 43-64. Providence, RI: Berghan.

Tanner, John F, Jr., Ellen Day, and Melvin R. Crask, 1989. Protection motivation theory: An extension of fear appeals theory in communication. *Journal of Business Research, 19*, 267-276.

U.S. News Story Page. Mass suicides in recent years. CNN. p. 2. Accessed December 29, 2005, from http://www.cnn.com/US/9703/27/suicide.list/index.html

WikiAnswers. (2009). Accessed January 26, 2009, from http://wiki.answers.com/Q/ what_percentage_of_Americans_have_access_to_the_internet_either_at_home_ or_at_work?

Yahoo!News. 2006. Deadline passes with no word of reporter (January 20), Reuters. Accessed January 20, 2006, from http://news.yahoo.com/fc/world/iraq.

Chapter Two

The Enthymeme as a Persuasive Device in Terrorists' Media Messages

A terrorist's message and fear go hand in hand. News from the Middle East (in the early decades of the twenty-first century) is filled with descriptions of terrorist activities directed against the West, Western sympathizers, Israelis and their supporters, and against one Islamic religious sect or another. News of terrorist activities often constitutes a substantial portion of daily news reports and reflects a cry of anger, defiance, challenge and argument in a diverse world of religion, politics, economics, and culture.

An emotion that permeates a terrorist's message (carried in the form of a news report) is fear. And, the idea resulting in fear becomes the logic behind the persuasive message. Where fear is the persuasive objective (or unintentional outcome) of a set of news messages, the result may consist of unpredicted consequences, in one form of irrational behavior or another. Fear is, first, individual and, second, collective.

Fear can have a stultifying effect on an individual, and people cope with fear in a variety of ways to bring stability to the disequilibrium caused by the fear. But, that specific fear may become common to a society, and, as with personal fear, societies seek coping mechanisms that strive to reduce the disequilibrium caused by the fear.

The nearly universal availability of messages on a global scale—generated by news organizations and the information and opinion pieces of the blogger—allows the fear-encased message to reach the thought processes of much of the world's population almost simultaneously. The purpose of this chapter is to suggest that the terrorist uses a variety of powerful persuasive fragments as a collage to drive home a subliminal message to viewers and readers of the jihadist's message.

It should be noted, first, that the terrorist act exists as an event that fits the journalistic news hole ideally. The news-generating action exists in the form of a brief, violent action that has personal consequences. For example, a beheading, a hostage taking, a suicide bombing are tailored to fit the event-oriented, time-constrained format of television news in particular and the event-oriented, space-constrained format of print journalism. The personal nature of the event (one person summarily taking the life of another, or a cartridge belt of explosive canisters slaying people indiscriminately) also resonates sympathetically with the journalistic desire to personalize the news story. In short, the ingredients of the terrorist act constitute a recipe for a high-interest news story.

The terrorist event contains high drama, is visually graphic, and is constrained in time. The entire story of a beheading or a suicide bomb explosion and its immediate aftermath or the seizing of a hostage at gunpoint can be told effectively as a story—with a beginning, a middle, and an end (to the event itself)—within the two-and-a-half minutes of a television news story. The terrorist event, because of its savagery and contradiction of basic Western values (and the values of nearly every other culture as well), is designed to trigger extreme emotions—anger, disgust, rage, and fear. The extreme emotion sends a persuasive message (usually intended to achieve some behavioral objective), but the extremeness of the emotion short-circuits the usual line of market-oriented persuasive appeals that incorporate fear as one element in a syllogistic message.

For example, a television commercial might use the relatively minor fear of social embarrassment as a premise in a syllogistic argument that encourages customers to buy a certain brand of dishwasher soap that won't leave spots on their glasses. The commercial might suggest that people with career aspirations would want to avoid social embarrassment. The minor premise suggests that presenting an image of excellence in social matters will suggest excellence in other areas of expertise as well. The conclusion is that the use of a certain product will allow one to avoid social embarrassment.

The persuasive structure of the argument combines a fear component with an extended logical problem-solution analysis. The emotion of fear and a progression of logical steps that will achieve problem solution intertwine to achieve behavior modification. The purchase of product X will eliminate social embarrassment. Typically, arguments with a fear appeal allow for an extension of the resolution through a series of progressive steps, each recognizable for what it is and each leading logically to the next conclusion.

The terrorist's persuasive message differs from that of the conventional advertiser's persuasive message that contains an all-encompassing fear component. The advertiser's message incorporates the elements of a complete categorical syllogism—major premise, minor premise, and conclusion. The terrorist's message functions as an enthymeme. Aristotle tells us that an enthymeme is an argument derived from premises that do not need to be stated (Rhetoric, 16. See also Aristotle, Posterior Analytics.). The frame of the argument still mandates a conclusion, as is the case with the classical syllogism. Enough information is provided in the frame so that a viewer or reader will be able to use the material (whether in textual, visual, or audio form) to generate a syllogistic foundation that allows for a filling in of the missing premise or premises from the data banks that give us our stereotyped conclusion in response to any situation that might generate a stereotypical response to a situation (see Berger and Luckmann, 1966, and Schwartz, 1973). Such a situation would tap into our typification schemes (see Berger and Luckmann, 1966) or the information packets that contain our stereotypes.

THE ENTHYMEME AS A TOOL OF PERSUASION

The method with which an argument is presented may contribute significantly to the power that it contains, regardless of whether it constitutes high fear arousal or some gradation of fear arousal through moderate to low. That method depends on whether the message is structured in the form of an enthymeme, whether a small segment of the message is omitted so that the listener has to fill in that segment mentally (and unconsciously). An enthymeme is a syllogism with a missing premise or conclusion. The receiver of the message (listener or reader) needs to fill in the information. Even though the filling in of information is unconscious, it requires mental exertion on the part of the receiver, thus committing that person to participation in the construction of the message. That participation means that the message becomes partially created by the receiver (listener or reader). If one creates a message, one commits his attitudes and values to lwhat he has created. Persuasion has become automatic, in a sense. This action illustrates the principle of mental closure in Gestalt psychology. Gestalt theory suggests that the brain is holistic, parallel, and analog, with self-organizing tendencies. The law of closure simply says that the mind adds missing elements to complete a picture.

Counterarguments to the terrorist's unidimensional argument (high fear appeal, with no verbal ideational elaboration) often adopt a syllogistic form and lend themselves to conscious or unconscious manipulation of the syllogism for maximal effect. One manipulative element that increases the power of an argument is the enthymeme. Land, the counterarguments of government, for example, often intentionally or unintentionally omit a premise or conclusion to require receiver fill-in of missing data.

The use of this "fill-in" principle in idea has its counterpart in speech. It is what Schwartz (1973) calls mnemonic speech. Work on phonemic restoration demonstrates that the brain can fill in phonemes not actually present in speech. Schwartz says,

> I record a sentence such as, "the state governors met with their respective leg-islatures convening in the capital city," cut out the "gisla" in"legislatures," and substitute a cough or some extraneous sound, a listener will *hear* the entire word when it is played in a proper context. He will hear both the complete word "leg-islatures" and the cough sound, Even though the "gisla" sound in *"legislatures"* is not physically present. (151)

President George W. Bush and Vice President Richard Cheney [2001-2008] used the enthymeme when presenting arguments about terrorism. The direct argument often ran along the line that America needs to shore up its defenses against terrorism. The Democrats are in disarray about their policy toward terrorism, whereas the Republicans are unified on their policy on ter-rorism. The listener is left to fill in the unstated conclusion (implication). It doesn't require a great leap of imagination, in this instance, to conclude that the electorate ought to vote in Republican political candidates.

The enthymeme is a powerful persuasive tool. Its power arises, first, from the fact that it includes enough information in its contention to channel the thought processes of the receiver of the message in the direction of thought of the sender of the message. The receiver is directed onto the general path and headed in the general direction intended by the sender. However, enough of the message is omitted so that the receiver can choose from a number of responses to fill in the blank spaces left by the ideational omissions inherent in the enthymematic argument. This diverging series of optional conclusions is noted both by Peirce (1960) and Lannigan (1995). Therefore, the modicum of free choice that the receiver (listener or reader) has gives the receiver some control over his response. The freedom to make decisions is an element of power.

The power of the enthymeme arises, second, from the fact that the receiver must fill in missing information in the argumentative construct. The energy required to fill in the missing blanks tends to commit the receiver to the message. By filling in the blanks, the receiver has committed himself to the message. The receiver has contributed some of his own thinking to the mes-sage, and one tends to commit oneself to what one has created (or shared in the creation). This doesn't mean that the receiver endorses the message. It just means that the receiver accepts the argument as a complete statement. Understanding has occurred. The attitudinal response to the message may be negative as well as positive. When discussing hot and cool media, McLuhan (1964) notes, "A hot medium is one that extends one single sense in 'high definition.' High definition is the state of being well filled with data" (22). A cool medium, on the other hand, is one of low definition. Little is given, and much has to be filled in by the listener. "Cool media are high in participation or completion by the audience" (McLuhan, 23). The enthymeme functions in much the same way as a cool medium. The requirement that the audience fill in a portion of the message contributes to the power of the enthymeme.

The pattern of the enthymeme has been extended to the documentary film, and the terrorist's video message functions in a similar manner. The general perception of documentary film, or video, is that the content appearing on the screen transparently represents world reality. However, the documentary image—as with any photographic image within a frame—is a constructed interpretation of actuality. Such a conclusion does not negate the essential veracity of the theme of the visual work as a whole or the validity of the argument being made. That argument is irrelevant to the discussion of the inherent persuasive characteristics of a picture within a frame.

Finnegan (2001) says that when an audience assumes naturalism in a photograph, it is engaging in an assumptive activity that represents the enthymeme. In Finnegan's words, "When the audience for documentary photography . . . assumes the naturalism of the photograph, it is tapping into an argumentative resource that I call the naturalistic enthymeme" (9). The argument here is that the audience fills in the omissions in the argumentative construction, using its own knowledge and experience. Finnegan argues that the viewer of a photograph fills in the blanks of the argument depicted in the photograph. The viewer of the photograph provides the missing data with the assumption that the image is real, that it represents what Searle calls "brute" facts (objects apart from man's interpretation of them). The viewer of the photographic image assumes that the image is a representation of something in the world (representational realism). The viewer assumes that the image in the photograph actually occurred before a camera at a certain time and place (ontological realism). In addition, the viewer assumes that the photographer captured the image with no intervention on his part (mechanical realism) (Finnegan, 2001 Winter, 9). Therefore, a photograph may be considered to be a visual argument to the extent that it contains the possibility of the naturalistic enthymeme.

The terrorist's photograph meets the requirements of the naturalistic enthymeme. It represents reality; it represents an event actually occurring in front of the camera at a particular time and place; and it represents an event captured by the camera with no intervention from the photographer. Therefore, the reality of the event is underscored dramatically. The viewer is then left with the obligation of filling in the "textual" omissions in the argument.

We develop our belief from the facts and pieces of the picture that we are given (the naturalistic enthymeme). The picture frames our belief. The picture that we get of the terrorist act gives us bits and pieces of the jihadist persuasive message. We get a premise about the power of the enemy. We get a premise about the intent of the enemy. We get a fragment (premise) about the determination of the enemy. We get a premise about the religious conviction of the enemy. But, the conclusion is not drawn for us in the persuasive arguments. The arguments don't point to a specific conclusion (a specific resolution). The unstated conclusion invites audience completion of the message in the member's own way. There is just enough focus in the message to channel the conclusion into a negative reaction, which, in turn, would result in negative behavior by the receivers (of a disparate variety) but all of which would result in a weakening of the American polity. The ultimate objective of the terrorist argument is to bring about an implosion of the dominant culture. But, many paths may lead to that end, and the paths are sketched hazily and are vague and translucent intentionally so that the American public can fill in the details that—out of fear—would lead to their ultimate demise.

Whereas Maslow's hierarchy of needs seems to hold sway in societies based on rational thought processes, it should be noted that the mind is flexible and can elevate almost any value to a state of primacy, which can become an obsession that will accept self-annihilation. As John Milton noted, "The mind is its own place, and in itself can make a heav'n of hell, a hell of heav'n" (1667, line 253). Of course, Milton wasn't referring specifically to suicide bombers or cult suicide pacts. Nevertheless, he is suggesting that the mind has an almost infinite capacity to shift its value scheme upon its own will. Therefore, it seems unwise to assume that Maslow's hierarchy of needs (which ascribes values to each of the five levels of physical and psychological need) is universal. People constantly use their power of rationalization to alter the value scheme suggested by Maslow.

As Stern (2003) notes, "Today, people are largely free to choose their own identities. Just as nations are largely imagined communities . . . so too is individual identity" (156). Stern adds that identity and identification are different concepts and that "[i]ndividuals must identify their identities" (156). She cites this as an important reason that some adherents of jihad become suicide bombers and that some avid anti-abortionist adherents murder doctors. The point here is that a mind obsessed by a cause can alter the order of Maslow's hierarchy. For example, the self-actualization level can become a basic need if a person feels himself as one with some cause. Self-sacrifice or murder becomes a means of self-realization. However, in general, Maslow's hierarchy of needs remains useful in developing persuasive messages for target audiences within rational societal structures.

FEAR AND PERSUASIVE MESSAGES

The term "fear," as it applies to terrorists and their actions, crosses the psychological boundaries of anxiety and fear. A distinction is usually drawn between anxiety and fear. Anxiety involves a sense of apprehension, distress, and a feeling of uneasiness that is not focused on a specific object. Anxiety occurs when a critical mass of stimulation and arousal is reached. Beyond that point, anxiety sets in.

Fear is associated with some particular object, such as a fear of snakes or a fear of heights. Of the biological conditions that elicit anxiety (over-stimulation, cognitive incongruity, and response unavailability), a difficult situation occurs that a person does not know how to handle (Kelvens, 1997 Spring).

As noted in chapter 1, fear may also be defined as an unpleasant feeling of perceived risk or danger; the perceived risk may be real or not. Fear may also arise from a feeling of extreme dislike of some conditions or objects. An example of such fear is a fear of darkness (Absolute Astronomy, 2005). People who experience extreme fear may commit irrational and dangerous acts.

The fear associated with the threat of terrorism, as perceived in the terrorist's persuasive messages, seems to combine fear of an object (the person of the terrorist, the convictions of the terrorist, and the intentions of the terrorist) with a state of elevated anxiety arising from uncertainty about ways to handle the perceived threat. This uncertainty may be manifested in different ways but tends to seek reliance upon the state to provide both the sword and the protective shield. The sword takes the form of offensive military actions against the perceived threat from groups such as al-Qaeda, the Taliban, Hamas, Hezbollah, and others. The shield takes the form of increased security measures at home, such as an increased military presence at points of domestic vulnerability and legislative modification intended to strengthen the protective legal shield against potential internal terrorist threats.

THE POWER OF THE ENTHYMEMATIC ARGUMENT

The enthymematic argument is different in its structure from the argument based on a complete syllogism. Technically, an enthymeme is a structure in which a missing premise must be filled in verbally to create a logical linguistic concept of the whole. Moreover, an enthymeme functions similarly to an abstraction in the visual arts where the mind must insert information into the scene to assume an interpretable picture or where some lines in a line drawing are missing, just enough so that the mind, with some effort, can fill in the missing information and visualize the picture as a whole. In some respects, an enthymeme is like a mosaic where information fill-in is necessary to provide a complete image.

The process of mental closure in Gestalt psychology states, simply, that the mind adds missing elements to complete a picture, when a few elements of that picture are missing. But, the way that the mind completes the picture is also significant. Even though filling in of information is unconscious, it requires mental exertion on the part of the receiver, thus committing that person to participation in the construction of the message (McLuhan, 1962, 41. See, also, McLuhan, 1964, 23.). That participation means that the message has been partially created by the receiver (listener or reader). If one shares in the creation of a message, one commits one's attitudes and values to it. This doesn't necessarily mean that the receiver comes to agree with the values of the message. It simply means that the image elements and their associated ideas interact vigorously in the mind of the receiver, tend to be retained there, and generate strong emotional reactions based on a comparison of the values reflected in the original message with the receiver's own values. If a logical solution to the value conflict doesn't seem possible, a chaotic status may remain in the mind—and that status leads to fear, frustration, and a desire to retreat behind an all-powerful leader brandishing a Herculean sword.

The persuasive appeal of the visual imagery released by the jihadists—whether in still photographs or videos—falls primarily into one of two opposite categories. It should be noted that not all jihadist groups employ exactly the same type of persuasive components. Al-Qaeda, for example, concentrates on power images interlaced with a suggestion of absolute control. Palestinian groups, on the contrary, rely heavily on images of victimization. However, the category of images covers the collective range of terrorist images. The first category shows the jihadist as an all-powerful, invincible controller. These pictures show heavily armed men (although women and children are sometimes included), often masked and arrayed in close-knit groups that suggest strength and solidarity. The images suggest power, brutality, and determination. Hooded executioners are arrayed behind a kneeling American prisoner garbed in an orange jumpsuit (reminiscent of the orange jumpsuits that prisoners at Guantánamo Bay have been forced to wear). Such images are characteristic of the brutal force that powers the engine of the Islamic resurgence. Al-Qaeda propaganda pictures are typical of image generation of this type.

The second basic category of visual images shows the Islamists as innocent victims of the brutality of others. Images used in Palestinian messages are typical of this persuasive approach. Pictures of injured children on a hospital bed and a Palestinian baby who had been decapitated by an Israeli rocket are typical of these visual images. The body of the decapitated baby is being handed from one Palestinian soldier to another. A picture of a Palestinian woman being attacked by an Israeli mob and a Palestinian woman, with her arms stretched out in supplication, bravely defying an oncoming Israeli bulldozer are other typical examples of the victimization theme of jihadist image-makers.

Several sub-themes provide a composite picture of the controller theme. The first sub-theme is the ritual beheading, with four or five heavily armed, hooded men with the victim kneeling in front of them and the black and white jihadist flag (in Arabic) on a wall behind the men. The stark, black-and-white flag reads," [t]here is no God but Allah, and Muhammed is His Prophet." The fact that the message on the flag is in Arabic is significant. No attempt is made to express the idea in a lingua franca—English, for example. Power and control are suggested by requiring others to recognize your language,

Figure 2.1. Intimidation and control through ruthless power are intended to generate fear of the enemy and generate a sense of safety and security for one's own people. The fear generated in the enemy is intended to destroy the enemy's resolve to resist an "irresistible force" and is a primary example of the controller theme in propaganda. The orange jumpsuit is a sign of revenge and stands as a metaphor for humility. This was the same type of orange jump suit that the Americans forced the detainees to wear at the Guantánamo Bay prison camp in Cuba. The inscription on the flag reads, "There is no God but Allah, and Muhammad is His Prophet."

Figure 2.2. A second powerful controller theme suggests the need for total societal commitment to the group's cause. This commitment may even include a mother's will-ingness to sacrifice her son in support of the cause. In this picture, a mother is bidding her son good-bye as he sets off on a suicide mission.

rather than theirs. Americans expect foreigners to communicate with them in English. Russians expect foreigners to communicate with them in Russian.

The second controller sub-theme involves children who are depicted as following in the footsteps of their elders as they learn the ritual of the Islamic jihadist or insurgent. Representative of this sub-theme is a child, with his face painted red, white, and green (in the colors of the Palestinian flag) aiming a submachine gun. Another image of the child soldier shows a column of boys marching (carrying a revolutionary banner and flags). A boy, with a rifle at port arms, is leading the march.

A third controller sub-theme involves the role of women in supporting the jihadist cause. Characteristic of this theme is a mother taking up arms as she bids goodbye to her 23-year-old son who is on his way to a suicide mission.

A fourth sub-theme involves the delight of the jihadist in the humiliation of the enemy. Typical of this sub-theme are the now-famous images of Palestin-ians cheering in wild celebration as they observe pictures of the toppling of the twin towers of the World Trade Center in New York on 9/11.

The double blow in dramatic enthymematic messages comes in the form of a concept that is diametrically opposed to the all-powerful controller—that is the weak, humble, abused victim. The combination of the all-powerful-controller image and the poor-abused-victim image is designed to weaken the will of the opponent as he empathizes with the victim. The purpose is to

Figure 2.3.   Jubilation at the defeat of a powerful enemy (through a highly successful, major terrorist attack) provides evidence of the effectiveness of one's power center and one's ability to humiliate the enemy. Such a propaganda device is a variation of the controller theme. This picture shows Palestinians rejoicing as they see pictures of the destruction of the Twin Towers of the World Trade Center in New York City, September 11, 2001.

Figure 2.4. Complementing the controller theme in propaganda is the victimization theme. The victimization theme is intended to create sympathy for the enemy by showing the enemy futilely resisting overwhelming force. The purpose of this propaganda theme is to create sympathy for the enemy and to soften the will of the aggressor in his determination to defeat the enemy at any cost. In this photograph, a Palestinian woman pleads with an oncoming Israeli bulldozer that is razing Palestinian olive groves. Victimization is created by showing brute, faceless force suppressing a defenseless opponent.

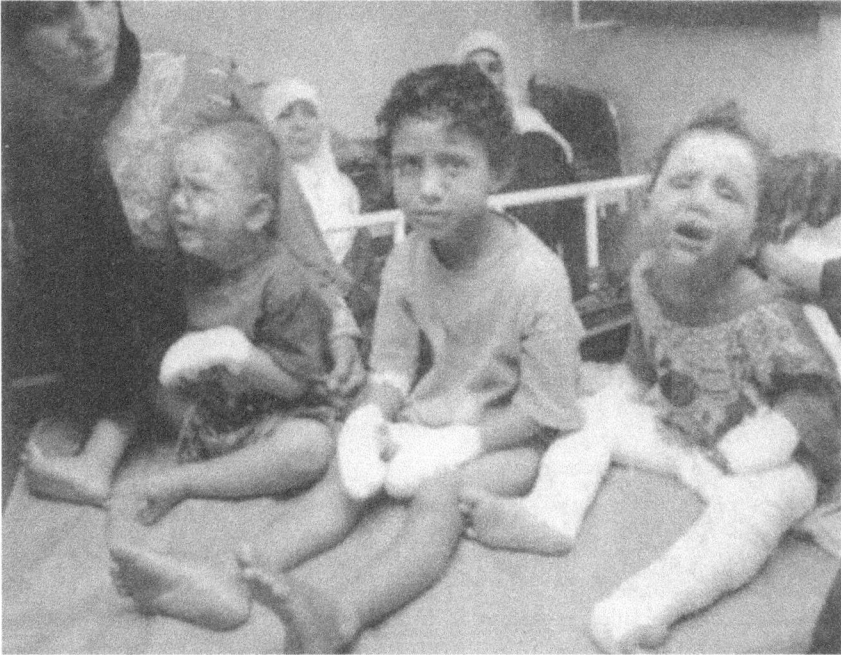

Figure 2.5. Victimization is often expressed most powerfully in the faces of helpless children. Here, three Palestinian children, injured in an Israeli raid, are seen, in agony, on a hospital bed.

diffuse the opponent's determination so that the imposition of the will of the controller will be an easier task. The objective is to gain the sympathy of the opponent so that the assertion of one's aggressive intent will face diminished roadblocks from a softened opposition.

Finnegan argues that the documentary image is a construction of reality. Its realism depends upon the expectations of the audience (its conventions and norms) that gives the documentary image a rhetorical thrust. The case is sometimes made that the documentary projects a fictional story; that is, there is a rhetorical dimension to the individual image and the sequence of images on the screen (Nichols, 1991). A similar case may be made for the newscast, which defines event significance and then which interprets event significance by what materials are put in the frame, how they are constructed within the frame, and how long they are developed as a representation of the day's events.

Whereas the documentary photograph taps the resource of the naturalistic enthymeme, so, too, the newscast requires an audience, oriented to the moment-by-moment visual world of the real day, to fill in the blanks of the

Figure 2.6. Victimization is expressed when the aggressor (as defined by the propagandist) is shown venting hatred and anger toward a member of the opposition. Victimization is intensified when the attack involves a personal assault on the victim. Here, a Palestinian woman is being personally assaulted by a group of Israelis. Such an image personalizes the hatred that is the major emotion fueling the two opposing political, religious, and cultural groups.

image on the screen to produce a composite picture that satisfies the sense of reality of the viewer. The viewer (or reader) helps create the argument being sketched within the video frame. As Finnegan (2009) states, "Thus photographs, and especially documentary photographs, may be considered to be visual arguments insomuch as they embody the possibility of the naturalistic enthymeme" (9).

A major concern of those defining the naturalistic enthymeme is the unconscious transference by the viewer of the image elements within the photographic frame to their world of reality. The terrorist image persuades enthymematically not only through the image elements within the frame, but also through the text of the message being presented. For example, a video released by Hamas showing a proud mother taking up arms beside her favorite son who is about to set out on a suicide mission argues that any sacrifice in the cause of Hamas is justified. The mother in the picture is supporting her son in a suicide mission. The implicit premise is that jihadist women, as well as men, must make an absolute sacrifice in the name of radical Islam.

Figure 2.7. Mutilation is another powerful victimization theme. Here, on Palestinian soldier hands the body of a baby, with its head blown off, to another Palestinian soldier. Such scenes are among the most dramatic possible in personalizing the concept of victimization.

The classic pre-beheading photograph, which shows hooded armed men arrayed behind a kneeling American in an orange jumpsuit, again persuades enthymematically as a textual message. The evident message is that the jihadist soldier is all-powerful. The minor premise is that the American is under the control of the all-powerful soldiers. The unstated conclusion that can be read into the evident visual premises is that radical Islam will bring America to its knees.

The emotional ripple effect of that conclusion is the ultimate objective of the creator of the persuasive message. America must defend itself in any way possible. The military theme of the message will likely direct the thought processes of the receiver of the message along such lines. Therefore, military responses, either offensive or defensive, become paramount in the mind of the receiver of the persuasive message. That line of thinking is consistent with the persuader's ultimate intent, which is to cause the implosion of the Western democracies.

Victim images also persuade enthymematically, as well a symbolically. The well-known image of a Palestinian boy shooting stones with a slingshot at Israeli tanks and soldiers suggests the helpless, innocent victim, defiant in the face of overwhelming odds. The major premise that is suggested by the visual imagery is that oppressed people must resist tyranny. A second premise in the picture is that Palestinians are oppressed people. The unexpressed conclusion is that even defenseless, oppressed people must struggle for their self-determination. The photograph of the boy with a slingshot not only persuades enthymematically, but it also persuades metaphorically. The boy suggests the biblical David in his struggle to defeat Goliath. Among the Hebrews, David was a genius, an insightful and shrewd military leader, a man of consummate discipline and control. He later became a ruler who had the ability to unite Israelites in one harmonious whole. And, he was a poet, who possessed and revealed a deep well of emotion, which poured forth in the Psalms. The image of the victim in the form of a hero of the enemy persuades both enthymematically and in unconscious metaphor. An extension of the victim theme hints that maybe that Palestinian boy is a David. Perhaps through the gifts possessed by David, the boy will become the savior of the Palestinians. Thus, the mnemonic elements of the persuasive image require that the viewer fill in the dots of missing information and meaning.

How enthymemes function, and the fact that they are an effective persuasive device, is well documented in the literature, but the reason that the enthymeme is a powerful persuasive device has not been well documented. Aristotle noted that some orators prefer examples to illustrate points in a speech and that other orators prefer enthymemes. Aristotle also observed that speeches that rely on enthymemes excite the louder applause (Rhetoric, 212).

That something in the enthymeme that magnifies the audience response in relation to the example lends persuasive impact to the enthymeme. It is possible that the difference in the impact of an example and an enthymeme concerns the way that the mind formulates a picture in relation to the way that picture elements are presented in each case. The example reveals picture elements gradually and systematically until the full picture (represented by the example) slides into place in the listener's (or reader's) mind. The enthymeme (with its characteristic of requiring the mind to fill in missing data instantaneously) has the greater impact because of the extra energy required in the fill-in process. The "aha" factor may give the enthymeme more dramatic impact than the example. By extension, the inherent drama in the terrorist's persuasive message is magnified through creation of an enthymematic statement.

Finally, it should be noted that the element of fear in persuasive messages is an important trigger that can cause a shift in attitudes, opinions, or beliefs. Its use in advertising messages usually kick-starts an action, but then the advertiser usually provides a picture of the path to be taken to reach the advertiser's desired objective. Although implication is often present, the advertiser's path to the target is logically formulated and laid out with a major and minor premise and a conclusion.

The terrorist's persuasive message truncates the three-part structure of a categorical syllogism by using a fear component as a syllogistic premise and leaving the conclusion in the form of a murky mosaic, the details of which need to be filled in by the receiver. That mosaic quality to the argument gives it its enthymematic character. The obligation on the part of the receiver to fill in the missing data mentally provides power to the argument.

The jihadist persuasive message, collectively, uses a carrot-and-stick strategy. The carrot is characterized by an image of Islamic victimization. The stick is characterized by an image of ruthless power. Whether constructed intentionally as enthymeme or not, the persuasive message of the jihadist has enthymematic force that contributes to its power to modify attitudes, opinions, and values. Therefore, the terrorist's message and fear are intertwined in an explosive ideational tool to promote the objectives of radical Islam.

REFERENCES

Absolute Astronomy. 2005. *Wikipedia,* June 14. Accessed January 6, 2007, from http://www.absoluteastronomy.com/encyclopedia/f/fe/fear.htm.

Aristotle, trans. 1960. *Posterior analytics.* In J. Tredennick (Trans.). Loeb Edition. Cambridge: Harvard University Press.

Aristotle, trans. 2005. *Rhetoric.* Trans. J.E.C. Welldon. www.elibron.com Elibron Classics, Adamant Media Corporation. Facsimile: 1886 Edition. New York: Macmillan.

Berger, Peter L., and Thomas Luckmann. 1966. *The social construction of reality: A treatise in the sociology of knowledge.* New York: Anchor Books.

Fear. 2005. Wikipedia, June 14. Accessed January 6, 2007, from http://absolute astronomy.com/encyclopedia/f/fe/fear.htm.

Finnegan, Cara A., 2001. The naturalistic enthymeme and visual argument: Photographic representation in the 'skull controversy.' *Argumentation and Advocacy,* Winter, 37(3),133.

Kelvens, Carissa. 1997. *Fear and anxiety,* Spring. Accessed January 6, 2007, from http://www.csun.edu/~vcpsy00h/students/fear.htm

Lanigan, Richard L. 1995. From enthymeme to abduction: The classical law of logic and the postmodern rule of rhetoric. In Lenore Langsdorf and Andrew R. Smith, eds. *Recovering pragmatism's voice: The classical tradition, Rorty, and the philosophy of communication.* Albany, NY: State University of New York Press.

Milton, J. (1667). *Paradise lost.* Ib, l.253.

McLuhan, Marshall. 1962. *The Gutenberg galaxy: The making of typographic man.* Toronto: University of Toronto Press.

———. 1964. *Understanding media: The extensions of man.* New York: McGraw-Hill.

Nichols, Bill. 1991. *Representing reality: Issues and concepts in documentary.* Bloomington, IN: Indiana University Press.

Peirce, Charles S. 1960. *Collected papers of Charles Sanders Peirce,* Vols.1-6. Cambridge: Harvard University Press.

Figure 2.1. (2006, November 27). *American beheading.* Accessed March 13, 2007, from http://archivofoto.blog.excite.it/img/AMERICAN-BEHEADING.jpg.

Figures 2.2-2.7. (2006, November 27). *Terrorism and the right to exist.* Accessed March 13, 2007, from http://newyorkjewishherald.com/terrorism_and_the_right_to_exist3.htm. The *New York Jewish Herald* disclaims any responsibility for this web site. Telephone call to the editorial department of the *New York Jewish Herald,* October 23, 2008.

Schwartz, Tony. 1973. *The responsive chord.* Garden City, New York: Anchor Press/ Doubleday.

Searle, John R. 1995. *The construction of social reality.* New York: The Free Press.

Stern, Jessica. 2003. *Terror in the name of God: Why religious militants kill.* New York: HarperCollins.

Chapter Three

Social Construction of Media-Generated Terrorist Images

An explosion is heard. A puff of smoke billows for a moment before dissipating. A storefront collapses under the weight of its ruptured timbers. Twisted metal obscures the identity of the cars parked along the street. Bloody bodies strew the street, including the body of the person who had a bomb attached to a belt under his tunic. Police and paramedic sirens are heard at a distance and then scream into the foreground. Privately owned camcorders, news cameras, and cell phone cameras record every moment of the scene. Another suicide bomber has struck again. Another terrorist event is poised to become international news. Another persuasive message is sent to societies everywhere. The image of the terrorist is reinvigorated in our minds. The fading texture of the image has been restored to high resolution. Another persuasive message has been sent for consideration by Western society.

Political intent, obsessive determination, the design of a media-friendly message (short, intense, graphic, shocking, morally repulsive), the use of fear in the persuasive message, and irrational appeals to emotion squelch any elaboration of the argument, and the knowledge that the message will be seen and heard in virtually every corner of the world—these are the characteristics of the terrorist's persuasive message. The terrorist also knows that a message constructed in this way will be very unlikely to suggest a logical path of thought that Westerners and their own populations might use to resolve the problems generating conflict between Islamic and Western societies. The originator of persuasive messages devises communication structures (words, images, ideas, motion, sound, feeling, color) in a way that will work on the unconscious mind of the enemy so as to encourage him to take irrational actions that will weaken the Western citizens' will to resist, will weaken the West's military will, will weaken the West's economic stability, and will erode the West's political unity in its effort to resist terrorism, ultimately causing the Western society to implode from its accumulated societal fractures.

Fear, as a component of persuasion, is used in a variety of types of messages designed to influence some population. Advertisers have been using a fear component in persuasive messages for some time, and advertisers, as well as academics, have been studying the role of fear in argument and how to incorporate a fear element most effectively in a persuasive message. Fear is the major (and, often, the exclusive) component of a terrorist's persuasive message, and the vehicle for conveying the message, through image and word, is primarily the mass media, increasingly including the internet.

The thesis of this chapter is that persuasion, in a terrorist's message, relies on the social construction of reality to create the image of an invincible enemy. However, the constituent elements in a terrorist's message need to be defined and differentiated from the constituents of an advertiser's message that also contains a fear component.

The terrorist's message benefits from the omnipresence and immediacy of mass communication. The terrorist's message benefits further from the nature of communication made possible by the internet. The terrorist's message is also characterized by the way in which persuasive elements—particularly the fear element—are assembled in a persuasive message. The terrorist's message benefits further from journalistic applications of the social construction of reality. Finally, the primary purpose of a terrorist act is to create news. This chapter will examine each one of these elements of terrorist messages.

Students of sociology are well aware of the nexus of communication channels and the neuronal brain paths that concentrate messages into the brain centers where message interpretation occurs. The web of the internet and our other message communication channels form something like an electronic skullcap that interconnects message senders, communication channels, and receivers in one subcutaneous neuronal network that connects the world to us and us to the world.

To enhance our understanding of the psychological workings of the mind, let us look briefly at the physical workings of the mind. It is probably significant that the physical nature of the communication channel in the brain allows for a speedy categorization of incoming data, storage of those data in memory packets in the unconscious mind, and allows for an almost instantaneous reintegration of those data into the conscious mind upon a related stimulus. All of the signal elements converge into a series of neurons (specialized cells of the brain and nervous system) that communicate via a relay system of electrical impulses and specialized molecules called neurotransmitters (NIH News, 1). Understanding the uniformity of neuronal activity in both the conscious and unconscious minds makes it a little easier to link the two often-opposed functions. The conscious and unconscious minds seem to be involved in a constant interplay of ideas, images, emotions, and values.

Audio loudspeakers, television screens, and computer screens connect with the nervous system's soma (the central bulb containing the nucleus of neural cells in the nervous system). The soma has both input and output channels, the dendrites and axons. Dendrites carry signal inputs; axons carry the output. We have immediate access to a single thread of the creation and decoding of a message—our conscious thoughts. However, thousands of other messages lie hidden within other regions of the brain. These message packets feed the meaning and emotional responses that we encode in response to a decoded message.

Audio signals displace air molecules in the form of sound waves. When these waves strike the eardrum, the waves create a vibration in the drum. This vibration is transferred mechanically through the middle ear bones. The mechanical energy is transferred to a liquid within the inner ear. An electric impulse is generated by nerve cells that line the cochlea. As the electric impulse moves through a neuron, it is converted into a chemical signal. The chemical signal is released into the gap between adjoining cells, where it stimulates the next neuron. Once again the signal becomes electrical and makes its way into the brain paths that provide our immediate conscious thought and the unconscious reservoir of our informational data, our attitudes, opinions, and values that reside in our memory banks. The point here is that the sources of conscious thought and unconscious image, meaning, and feeling consist of the same form of electrical activity. Therefore, electrical activity seems to be the common bond of both conscious and unconscious thought.

When we think of the electrical nature of mass communication and the corresponding electrical character of message flow and meaning formulation in the meaning reservoirs of the brain, the image of an electronic skullcap is fairly accurate. That is, we are plugged in to the information channels of the world in much the same way that many people these days are plugged in to an iPod or an MP3 player.

Information input is almost constant and, therefore, generates an almost constant demand for a corresponding interrelation between the conscious and unconscious sides of ourselves. We seem to have reached the point, which Marshall McLuhan (1964) predicted half a century ago, "We have extended our central nervous system itself in a global embrace, abolishing both space and time as far as our planet is concerned" (3). The electronic skullcap analogy of a moment ago is congruous with McLuhan's further observation:

Rapidly, we approach the final phase of the extensions of man—the technological simulation of consciousness, when the creative process of knowing will be collectively and corporately extended to the whole of human society, much as we have already extended our senses and nerves by the various media. (3-4)

However, the addition of the internet changes the equation somewhat regarding the way that we process and respond to messages. Prior to the widespread use of the internet, messages, in general, went through some sort of filtering process—an editor at the desk of a newspaper or magazine or a peer review committee evaluating a manuscript. Although not a perfect process, the screen slowed message flow and provided a modified perspective on the nature of the messages. Time for reflection usually modified the intensity (and, sometimes, the direction) of the emotional component in a response. In addition, an edited message often refines its ideational content so that it directs the thought inherent in the message to one chamber of factual content in the memory banks rather than another. Of course, much content on the internet consists of edited material from established news organizations, but the vastly expanded capacity of the internet allows for a large amount of unedited lay opinion.

Whether altering the vector (the velocity and direction) of the message is good or bad is debatable. However, the effects of unfiltered messages can be seen in the way that many people respond to messages on the internet. Friedman (2005) observes that the "flat world," as he calls it, "enables small acts—the killing of just a few people—to have big effects" (431). However, political theorist Yaron Ezrahi says, "The new system of diffusion—the Internet—is more likely to transmit irrationality than rationality. Because irrationality is more emotionally loaded, it requires less knowledge, it explains more to more people, it goes down easier" (cited in Friedman, 2005, 432).

The internet eliminates the previously required filter in the message chain, and, with the filter gone, people, eager for instant gratification of their beliefs, can achieve that gratification online. Instant gratification of one's emotional mindset allows for an intensification of the emotion and decreases the likelihood that reflection will expand the process of thought. Friedman reinforces this view when he says, "Young people used to take LSD to escape. Now they just go online. Now you don't shoot up, you download. You download the precise point of view that speaks to all your own biases" (432).

TERRORISTS' USE OF PERSUASION

Terrorists perform violent acts primarily as persuasive messages. The immediate effect of a violent act, such as a beheading, is to realize a persuasive objective. The primary objective is fear. Fear, in many ways, is a strange objective. It has subtle overtones. Fear creates an image of the enemy. That image is of an invincible warrior at your doorstep. That invincible warrior can exercise complete control over your life. You must follow his will—and his every word—or your life will be extinguished. This isn't subtle, indirect control; it is immediate, direct, and absolute control over your life. There is nothing very subtle here.

Terrorists use this direct access to the brain—figuratively described as an electronic skullcap—by sending messages depicting their terrorist act to nearly everyone around the globe via the internet and then seeking access to established news organizations. Their actions, such as a beheading, a hostage taking, or a suicide bombing, are tailored to fit in the event-oriented, time-constrained format of television news in particular, as well as in the event-oriented, space-constrained format of print journalism. The terrorist's purpose is (1) to reestablish his image in the minds of all societies (friend and foe alike)—to refresh the focus on the man and his character, (2) to send an impactful persuasive message to the enemy's society, and (3) to serve as a persuasive recruiting device for his own society (another facet of the terrorist's persuasive purpose).

The ideational content of the terrorist's message is fairly simple; the logic is enthymematic (see chapter 2). The ideas of conservative Islam must prevail and become persuasive. The sword will ensure the imposition of the message. And, then there is a twist. The conclusion of the message is not an idea per se (thus the enthymematic character of the message). Rather, the propagandist hopes that the fear generated by the truncated message will cause a conservative knee-jerk reaction in the enemy society that will cause that society to take action that, ultimately, will weaken the society and will make it vulnerable to attack with a fractionated fabric and weakened will to resist.

In brief, an enthymeme is a syllogism (major premise, minor premise, and conclusion) in which a premise is omitted, requiring the listener (or reader) to fill in the missing idea from his store of schemas and stereotypes. This action generates emotion, which gives the argument more impact than it would have if it were a fully fleshed out construction of logic.

The weakening could arise from the economic impact of inordinate expenditures for defense and homeland security. The weakening could arise from the erosion of political will within the enemy society in the face of military casualties or repeated politico-military setbacks (degradation of efforts to win the "hearts and minds" of the populace in the regions occupied by insurgents). The weakening could arise from the fractionating and subsequent weakening of the value and belief system of the enemy country, with a corresponding loss of a focused societal purpose.

Therefore, the persuasive purpose of the terrorist is not to orchestrate a specific action (to buy a specific brand of automobile) or to orchestrate an attitude to create a mindset that will predispose future action in one direction rather than another (to favor and vote for Republican candidates, rather than Democratic candidates, at the next election). The persuasive purpose of the terrorist is to create fear, with the nebulous objective of dividing and softening an enemy society so that it will implode or become easy prey for a once-weaker opponent.

The collective psychological studies of fear suggest that fear may constitute a legitimate component in a persuasive message. However, most advertisers' persuasive messages consist of a combination of cognitive components (rational thought) and (at times) a fear component (an irrational emotional impulse). A persuasive message constructed in a logical manner usually has information that suggests paths to the solution of a problem. A fear element may help create a felt need for action. However, other cognitive elements of the message indicate the path for problem solution. That path is based on logical thought processes.

The terrorist's persuasive message muddies (or virtually eliminates) cognitive components and—like enthymematic thinking in argumentative structure—leaves the receiver of the message to supply his own idea as a conclusion to an open-ended portion of the syllogism. The social construction of reality is particularly important in the consideration of the way in which the receiver of a terrorist's persuasive message fills in the nebulous or missing premise or conclusion of an irrational persuasive message. The material filled in is based on image and one's interpretation of the meaning of that image. That is where the social construction of reality enters this discussion.

THE SOCIAL CONSTRUCTION OF REALITY

Social construction of reality tells us that an individual, in varying degrees, is molded by his social relations. Social construction theory borrows heavily from phenomenology, a philosophy based on the premise that reality consists of objects and events as they are perceived or understood in human consciousness and not anything independent of human consciousness. Berger and Luckmann (1966) suggest, "Men *together* produce a human environment, with the totality of its socio-cultural and psychological formations" (51). Specifically, a social construct "is an institutionalized entity or artifact in a social system 'invented' or 'constructed' by participants in a particular culture or society that exists solely because people agree to behave as if it exists, or agree to follow certain conventional rules" (Social Construction. 2006, 1). Our sense of self is shaped by the language we use, the type of education that we are exposed to, and the norms and values that we learn at home, among our peers, as a part of teams, in school, at work, at church, and within our social groups.

Somewhere in the memory banks of the brain, mentioned earlier, lie the stocks of social knowledge that Schutz (1967, 1970) said allow us to make sense quickly of what goes on around us and then allow us to structure our actions accordingly. Based on the principles of phenomenology, Schutz said that this collection of mindsets allows us to navigate life with relative ease— with little effort and thought.

The existence of typifications in our memory banks allows us to classify objects and actions that we observe and develop instantaneous response patterns to them. Such snap judgments save time and effort. They obviate the necessity of constructing a pattern of logical thought process to give meaning to our observations. Because much of our observation requires us to develop meaning in relation to what we observe, having to undergo full logical processes of thought each time some meaning is called for would bog down the mind in tiring and time-consuming delays. The ability of the brain to respond to moment-by-moment problems confronting us would diminish. Efficiency of living would be lost. But, the downside to this efficiency is that the typification that springs forth (from the unconscious store of images, attitudes, and beliefs) can also distort our understanding of the experience. Bias results. Actually, Berger and Luckmann extend the incipient concept of typification into the broader concept of social roles. As noted, this chapter limits the concept of typification to its more elemental aspects, which relate closely to the stereotypical image per se.

The meaning, belief, attitude, and value packets that reside in the recesses of the brain refer to what Berger and Luckmann call typification schemes (Berger and Luckmann, 1966). These are collections of meanings that we give to some phenomenon. These meanings derive from the stock of knowledge that we have acquired socially. That knowledge allows us to place the phenomenon in a context that gives us comfort, a sense of rightness about the world around us, and a sense of closure to the mental disquiet.

Berger and Luckmann (1966) remind us that we attach a meaning to our environment that is *subjective* rather than *objective*. These become *signs*—objects designed "to serve as an index of meaning" (35). In elaboration on the function of typifications in human thought processes, Berger and Luckmann say,

> Habitualization provides the direction and the specialization of activity that is lacking in man's biological equipment, thus relieving the accumulation of tensions that result from undirected drives. And by providing a stable background in which human activity may proceed with a minimum of decision-making most of the time, it frees energy for such decisions as may be necessary on certain

occasions. In other words, the background of habitualized activity opens up a foreground for deliberation and innovation. (53)

Once we understand that we are responding to signs with triggered reactions from typification schemes, we begin to realize the importance of the people and institutions which influence a culture's definitions of its symbols and signs and construct the typification schemes into one pattern rather than another. The mass media play a major role in this process, because they transmit the image and idea of the culture of which they are a part, and they frame that image to provide the most graphic and accurate interpretation of that culture. The image of our own culture becomes the "we" interpretation. The counter-image associated with the other culture creates the "they" interpretation of the relationship.

There is a direct path of development from the theoretical principles of the social construction of reality and the generation of image in advertising, marketing, and public relations. For example, a study by Van Zoonen (1992) adopted a "social constructionist" approach in relating media to events associated with the women's movement. She notes, "In . . . a *social constructivist* perspective . . . media play a more important and complex role than that of plain transmitters of movement messages and activities. Media will select certain issues and activities for coverage while ignoring others" (456). Van Zoonan adds, "It is not the *transmission* of certain selected items which is at stake, but a particular *construction* of the movement's ideas and activities" (456). The selection process within the news editorial office results in the shape of the image that will be projected of the organization. Van Zoonen notes further, "The media image of the movement is the result of an intricate *interaction* between movement and media," (456) that leads to a certain *public identity* and *definition*.

The question of image and man's actions based on attitudes and opinions associated with the image are closely correlated with observations of early mass media specialists. And, these observations parallel closely the ideas of social constructionists. For example, Walter Lippmann (1922) spoke of the importance of the "pictures in our heads" that arise from reported descriptions of events that we have not experienced directly. Lippmann says, "Looking back we can see how indirectly we know the environment in which nevertheless we live. We can see that the news of it comes to us now fast, now slowly; but that whatever we believe to be a true picture, we treat as if it were the environment itself" (4). Consistent with the belief of the social construction of reality is Lippmann's observation, "The only feeling that anyone can have about an event he does not experience is the feeling aroused by his mental image of that event" (9).

The image that arises in our minds is a fiction, but it is a fiction that we need to have to give us the satisfaction, the mental quiet, that we need to maintain a psychological equilibrium. Lippmann says, "The fiction is taken for truth because the fiction is badly needed" (12). Lippmann goes on to say that people seldom act on direct and certain knowledge; rather, people act on the pictures that have been created for them. The vast majority of these pictures come from the mass media.

One reason that the nature of an image is important and needs to be studied seriously lies not only in our desire to understand the truth per se, but also because much important political action—particularly in a democracy—is dependent upon public opinion. As Edward Bernays (1929) noted, when he was crystallizing the theoretical ideas underlying public relations, "Perhaps the most significant social, political, and industrial fact about the present century [twentieth century] is the increased attention which is paid to public opinion, not only by groups or movements that are dependent on public support for their success, but also by men and organizations which until very recently stood aloof from the general public and were able to say, 'the public be damned'" (34).

One element in the focusing of public opinion is the creation of images that can serve the purpose of the persuader. These images may function as part of the persuader's message or—in the case of a terrorist's message—become the argument itself. Bernays recognized the significance of typifications when he noted, "Mental habits create stereotypes just as physical habits create certain definite reflex actions. These stereotypes or reflex images are a great aid to the public relations counsel in his work. These short-cuts to reaction make it possible for the average mind to possess a much larger number of impressions than would be possible without them" (162).

TYPIFICATIONS AS STEREOTYPES

Although the stereotype is often thought of as a contrived bias that one invokes consciously in an effort to denigrate another, the stereotype should rather be understood as a culturally imbued concept that has receded into the unconscious of an individual or a society to provide an almost instinctual fight-flight response to some stimulus. A stereotype may arise from a limited experience with a person, an event, a place, or an object or from dialogue in one's cultural community.

The stereotype that enters the unconscious mind through the society may arise from an experience with an object. A caveman, for example, might see a Tyrannosaurus eagerly devour for lunch a careless comrade whose curiosity

took him too close to the animal's forbidding teeth. The surviving caveman
learns very quickly that the huge carnivore with serrated teeth that walks on
two legs must be avoided at all costs. This message becomes conveyed to the
society at large. Associated with the message is a feeling of fear, hatred, and
loathing. The emotion is associated with the image. The next time that the
caveman sees a Tyrannosaurus, a quick, non-logical, emotion-related image
springs into the caveman's mind. There is no time for a logical progression
of thought. The emotion readies the body for action; the scary image triggers
defensive behavior. Upon sighting a Tyrannosaurus, a member of the cave
culture doesn't have to pause for observation or go through a protracted logical analysis. The sight of a Tyrannosaurus means run away fast.

On the other hand, another caveman [there is a difference in geologic time
periods here] might see a Brachiosaurus wandering about munching on tree-
tops. A curious comrade walks by the Brachiosaurus (not close enough to be
stepped on or to enrage the animal) and lives to describe the wondrous event.
The observing caveman concludes that one can coexist with such animals (if
you don't get too close). That information becomes imbued in the culture, and
the cave society learns to respond, without thought or extended observation,
that one doesn't have to run away from a Brachiosaurus. (Just don't get close
enough to be stepped on.) The short-circuited image of the Brachiosaurus
might include the associated emotions of mild alarm, attentiveness, no fear,
and neutral emotions. The nearly instantaneous conclusion of the caveman
(drawing on his stereotype) is that this monster is not a direct threat to me. If
I mind my own business, I can coexist with this creature.

In each case, information becomes internalized and packaged for immediate release in the form of a conclusion (run fast) rather than in the form of a
proposition (I need to evaluate this Tyrannosaurus anew to determine its characteristics). Therefore, the stereotype becomes a time and energy efficient
device that allows the holder of the stereotype to protect himself, register his
belief in regard to the person, object, place, or thing in question and return to
a state of mental equilibrium as soon as possible.

Of course, a stereotype can short-circuit thought at a time that can become
destructive in the relationship of the prejudiced individual, place, or thing and
the person or object that is subject to prejudice. However, this truncated im-
age-belief packet in the mind may have positive, as well as negative, effects
in the nature of the interaction of people or groups. A stereotype, therefore,
refers to a particular kind of response (jumping to a conclusion), which may
have either negative or positive overtones.

The stereotype is a concept that may or may not be useful; therefore, "The
public relations counsel sometimes uses the current stereotype, sometimes
combats them and sometimes creates new ones. In using them he very often

brings to the public he is reaching a stereotype they already know, to which he adds his new ideas, thus he fortifies his own and gives a greater carrying power" (Bernays, 1929, 162-163). It was almost a century ago that Bernays (1929) said, "Domination to-day is not a product of armies or navies or wealth or policies. It is a domination based on the one hand upon accomplished unity, and on the other hand upon the fact that opposition is generally characterized by a high degree of disunity" (133).

Therefore, some events are interpreted—and other events are created—with a persuasive objective that incorporates—or is sometimes dominated by—a fear element. These messages, time and again, top our typification schemes and heighten the visual resolution of our image of the enemy. To develop a stereotype of the enemy in an armed conflict is a primary objective of many persuasive messages.

People's curiosity about people, places, things, and events has many similar characteristics. That is the reason that people are interested in information that flows from an actual news event or information that flows from a contrived news event, what Daniel Boorstin described as a pseudo-event (see Boorstin, 1961). The value of an event is heightened (some say created) by the fact that it is covered by newspapers, magazines, radio, and television, and that it fills the space of bloggers' Weblogs.

Media coverage of an event is largely what makes it news. As Boorstin (1961) says, "It is the report that gives the event its force in the minds of potential customers. The power to make a reportable event is thus the power to make experience" (10). According to Boorstin, a pseudo-event has four characteristics: First, "It is not spontaneous, but comes about because someone has planned, planted, or incited it" (11). (An earthquake constitutes a spontaneous event; an interview would usually fall under the category of a contrived event.) Second, "It is planted primarily (not always exclusively) for the immediate purpose of being reported or reproduced" (11). (Its occurrence is arranged for the convenience of the media, and its success is measured by how widely it is reported.) Third, "Its relation to the underlying reality of the situation is ambiguous" (11). (The interest of an event is stimulated by this ambiguity. What can the terrorists hope to achieve by beheading this journalist?) And, fourth, "Usually it is intended to be a self-fulfilling prophecy" (12). (Showing a terrorist group performing acts of violence makes violence an expectation within that group.)

The self-fulfilling prophecy associated with image is an integral part of the image of the terrorist shaped in the West, as well as the self-image of the terrorist shaped within the terrorist's own culture. (The Islamic terrorist is the most prominent in the first decade of the twenty-first century, but the terrorist's self-image is characteristic of any terrorist group.)

Boulding (1956) emphasizes the importance of image feeding upon itself. "That part of the relational image which deals with the relations among persons is peculiarly subject to strange dynamic instability arising out of the fact that persons themselves are to a considerable extent what their images make them" (71). Personal relations involve a complex set of actions and reactions, with one image interacting with another in a kaleidoscopic pattern of change, reinforcement, or deterioration of the interchanged images. Boulding notes, "Because the image is a creation of the message people tend to remake themselves in the image which other people have of them" (71).

In a prescient observation that predated the irrational terrorist actions of Islamic extremists (in the early twenty-first century), Boulding says that the impact of society on the image is most important in the value image. He argues that acquired values can dominate biological values that exist in the form of hunger, thirst, pain, fear, and sex. Then, Boulding says, "The specific forms which these drives take, however, are elaborated and varied almost beyond belief by the baroque processes of acculturation. Indeed, what might be called the acquired values in many cases dominate the biological ones" (72). He goes on to state that survival is not the highest human value. This perhaps helps explain the mindset of the kamikaze and the suicide bomber. "One suspects," says Boulding, "that survival is frequently a byproduct of the play of genetic forces. It is by the willingness to risk death that both men and animals gain life" (72).

In considering the importance of image in society, one should remember that the shapers of the cultural image of the society are usually those that have an invested interest in the status quo—particularly business interests, financial interests, and governmental interests. It is, of course, possible that other interests may play a role in the image- and value-shaping process, but only to the extent that they can begin to exercise some influence in that image- and value-shaping process. Major movies constitute one example of a possible countervailing interest.

The Terrorist Act as a Source of News

The terrorist act is a very effective vehicle for generating news coverage, because the event fits neatly into the Western news frame. It can be reported on briefly; it is dramatic; and it fits the we-they duality of a conflict between opponents. This telling of a story within rigid time or space constraints results in a distortion of the scope and nature of the terrorist, but such distortion often occurs because media coverage is reactive rather than anticipatory. Western media rely on an event-oriented, rather than idea-oriented, concept of journalism. Individuals or groups wanting access to the media have learned to create pseudo-events.

The expectation that it is events that constitute news keeps reporters from exploring trends in social problems and putting problems and events in some context. "As a result," Picard (1993) says, "audiences, including authorities, are forced to confront terrorism at the micro rather than the macro level. This makes it possible for authorities to argue that society must deal with the manifestations of social problems—that is, the acts of terrorism and their effects—rather than the social problems themselves" (112).

The most important sources for foreign news in the United States are the agencies of the federal government, in particular the White House, the State Department, and the Pentagon. These agencies manage the flow of news about foreign countries that arises from an international crisis. Information is sometimes withheld—as may be the case with civil rights violations—or released selectively to a small group of "authorities," which, in turn, release the information through journalistic interviews. The selective release of information is common in response to reports of terrorism. The public gets the information from television or the newspapers from authorities whose most up-to-date information has come from the government (see Lang and Lang, 2000).

The corresponding news story is developed as a crisis—often involving opposing antagonists—and generates fear, which the government attempts to allay through demonstrating its strength and competence. Lang and Lang (2000) state, "Television news, even more than newspapers, has generally been driven by crisis, conflicts, and disaster, a pattern also manifest in news that comes from abroad" (300). In recent years, terrorism should be added to the list. Also, in recent years, the forces just cited driving news might be applied to the BBC World News and the international edition of Deutsche Welle (German broadcasting).

Altheide (1997) suggests that the problem frame used by the media to discuss issues, both in news and entertainment formats, is a major factor in producing societal fear. Framing is a process by which images and sounds are constructed selectively to focus the audience member's attention on one set of images, as opposed to another—much as the frame of a picture focuses the interest and attention on the content within the picture. The purpose may be aesthetic or persuasive or both. Framing refers both to selection of the content to be included in the frame and the juxtaposition of the content within the frame. That which lies outside of the frame is excluded from the field of view and, therefore, allows for the full concentration of the viewer's attention and interest on the content within the frame. This controlled structure of an image creates an impression that gives a picture of society from the perspective of the controller—thus being a part of the social construction of reality.

Much media programming deals with issues, but the issues are usually cast as "problems." A "problem" fits more neatly in the narrative storytelling structure of both news and entertainment programming than does the examination of an issue in the more loosely structured discussion-resolution format. Altheide says, "The problem frame promotes a discourse of fear that may be defined as the pervasive communication, symbolic awareness and expectation that danger and risk are a central feature of the effective environment" (648).

It should be noted that the creation of fear is subject to social influence. Society teaches people to worry about subjects such as money, status, sin and salvation, personal relationships, health, crime, and obesity (Altheide, 1997). Even though the target of fear is socially constructed, it is perceived as "real" and, therefore, has consequences. Social interaction and communication, including mass communication, provide the foundation for fear. And, the fear that is of primary concern to the sociologist concerns an anxiety held in common in a community, not an individual fear (see Altheide, 1997). Such is the case with the terrorist message.

The creation of fear needs to be associated with an enemy, and an enemy can be defined most concretely by creating a dichotomous image. The dichotomous image is created verbally by use of words such as "we" versus "they." Coloring in of the negative image occurs through reference to "evil" (or the "evil empire"), "demons," or, euphemistically, "those people." A nation needs "enemies" (see Merskin, 2004). A government uses the idea of a common enemy as a method of social control, a method of reinforcing the political, economic, and cultural values of the nation and as a mechanism for reinforcing those beliefs (see Keen, 1986; Spillman and Spillman, 1997). A common enemy can distract attention from other issues that a government might want to obscure. In addition, a common enemy allows for the creation of survival strategies that are grounded in the value and belief system of a nation. The United States has taken several major steps to consolidate information-gathering authority, police power, and broad-based physical security efforts since 9/11.

Let's narrow the focus on those specific aspects of the social construction of reality that set the stage for journalistic applications of these principles. Our sense of self is shaped by the language we use, the type of education to which we are exposed, and the norms and values that we learn at home, among our peers, as part of teams, in school, at work, at church, and within our social groups. The thinking, acting, reacting self is shaped largely through our relations with other people. These relations gradually shape our sense of identity and individuality (see Littlejohn, 2002; Croteau and Hoynes, 2003). The social construction of reality is not an argument per se, of course. That is, it does not structure words and images into a purposeful syllogism, as a carefully constructed verbal argument might (an argument about adopting American-style democratic principles or adopting ethanol as an alternative fuel for our cars). Nevertheless, the media frame words and images in such a way so that one image, instead of others, is created on the screen (or on the screen of the mind) and so that one set of words instead of others is created for our aural consciousness. Those images and words reflect one set of values, as opposed to others. They reflect one set of beliefs, as opposed to others. They express one economic philosophy, as opposed to others. They express one political perspective on the world, as opposed to others. They express one perspective on social organization, as opposed to others. They reflect one cultural perspective on the world, as opposed to others.

Consciously or unconsciously, the material that takes shape within the frame of the television screen or the "screen" of the journalist's column assumes the character of an argument. When we depict the world from the perspective of our own experience with the world and our own beliefs about the world, we are projecting an argument (intended or unintended). Therefore, the presentation of images from opposing world perspectives becomes a debate on the stage of world opinion. That debate is charged once opposing images are aired. Therefore, the construction of reality on a media screen positions the sparring opponents for the ensuing verbal and image battle.

As Littlejohn (2002) notes, "virtually any aspect of human experience can be viewed from the perspective of how it is made and used in the social construction of reality" (165). The resources for the social construction of reality include ideas, values, stories, symbols, meanings, institutions, and whatever else may be used to build a reality. These collected elements contribute to the perceptions that we hold of the world around us. Although perceptions aren't the total sum of reality, we act on our perceptions, thus making them a real part of existence. The resources for the social construction are shared with other people. Therefore, the values that become associated with our images and ideas are constructed jointly through interaction in society.

Littlejohn (2002) says that when a person looks at an object that was designed by people who interacted to bring that design into fruition, one is using communication in the construction of that reality. He cites, as an example, "architecture [which] is a form of expression in which designers, builders, and users make a certain social world. The cultures of the world differ substantially in how they express their values and beliefs through the kinds of buildings and homes they make" (165).

JOURNALISTIC APPLICATIONS OF
THE SOCIAL CONSTRUCTION OF REALITY

The social construction of reality is reflected very specifically in news story construction. It is the communication practices of journalists that shape facts into ways that they are perceived. Two characteristics of journalistic reporting create the journalistic fact. First, journalists seldom have the resources or access to the information pool of their sources in order to determine facts independently. Second, the principle of objectivity encourages the use of opposing accounts from sources with opposing viewpoints. As Ericson (1998) notes, "Journalists visualize the fact value of a story on the basis of a source's face value as an authoritative, normative witness to events" (1).

It is often said that television's pictures don't lie. Whereas there is no suggestion that lying is intended, news story construction in television also builds an image of reality that reflects the characteristics of the genre. The visual narrative of television directs attention to objects within a frame, uses staged news events, retakes, reenactments, and stock footage to construct a story. The television news story takes on literary value and blurs distinctions between fact, value, information, and knowledge. In short, "like literary fiction, news requires the willing suspension of disbelief in order to have its knowledge accepted" (1).

Communication plays a role in creating our perception of reality and in changing our perception of the nature of reality. The genre-specific elements of television influence the selection of items for a newscast. The categories into which news is defined place news into interpretive frames. News is divided into categories, such as politics, the economy, foreign affairs, domestic news, business, and sports. These categories determine what will be in the frame and the types of items that will be in a newscast as a whole (Chandler, 2005).

To make facts come alive, journalists provide visual representations of the facts. News accounts visualize an event, the reason something happened, what it was like to be involved, a possible solution to the associated problem, and a suggestion as to whether the event was good or bad (Ericson, 1998). The value dimension of news reporting leads reporters to look for that which disturbs behavioral norms, that which disturbs the status quo. A norm may be a factual standard in science, such as a risk threshold for environmental pollution, but it also functions as an ethical constraint. A moral evaluation is usually implied.

Several observers suggest that there is a bias toward dominant or consensual values, the underlying values of a given society. Stuart Hall has suggested that the media tend to reproduce symbolically the existing institutional power structure (see Chandler, 2005). Justin Lewis (1991) contends that television news "favours and sustains the hegemony of those with power" (12). He cautions that such a tendency may not reflect a conspiracy; rather, it is the product of a variety of social and semiotic determinations. Hall suggests that, over time, news helps create the consensus knowledge that reporters recognize as being newsworthy (see McQuail, 1987). Fiske (1987) says that a powerful force in the reading of a news text assumes that society should run smoothly, be law-abiding, and harmonious. The norms of a society are prescriptive and reflect the ideology of the dominant classes.

Briefly, *semiotics* refers to a relationship among a sign, an object, and a meaning. For example, the word *cat* causes us to picture a certain class of animals. Susanne Langer (1942) suggests that a sign corresponds closely to the signified object. A symbol doesn't just provide a mental picture of the object; it is a vehicle for the conception of objects. That is, a symbol allows us to process the sign and to incorporate relevant information that is not generated directly by the impression of the sign.

Much journalistic "fact" is derived from using credible sources. The statements from these sources are then quoted as fact. Source credibility is determined through institutionalized forms of authority and knowledge. There is heavy reliance on politicians and representatives of law enforcement agencies.

A news story can be made more compelling if it is cast in the form of a conflict between two opposing parties, what is sometimes referred to as a binary-opposition format. If research reveals that one side should be disconfirmed, the story would disappear. In turn, seeking out the opposing viewpoint provides the oppositional tension that lends drama to a news story.

Journalists frame events on the basis of their definition of news. News is that which disrupts the status quo. Therefore, that which is deviant becomes newsworthy. Ericson (1998) says, "Normal crime is not news; only abnormal crime is. If there is no deviance, there is no story" (5).

It is often claimed that the pictures of television make news in that medium more believable than in newspapers or on radio. The viewer can assess directly the moral character and authority of sources. Moreover, television images also appear to be happening in real time, thus reflecting the present tense. The construction of television news includes the staging of sources in ways to enhance the appearance of their authority. The work ethic is suggested peripherally by staging authorities in offices, with books and computers at hand, with documents piled on a desk, and in proper uniform. Perspective is determined by camera position. In covering a riot in which a phalanx of police confronts rioters, cameras are usually authorized behind police lines. This provides a view of the rioters from the perspective of the police. It suggests that the police are invincible and constitute the shield that protects the viewer from the chaos beyond.

Because footage shot live may not always suffice to tell the full visual story, television journalists often resort to what they refer to as fakes—retakes, reenactments, and the use of stock footage. Therefore, news items are not just selected but also actively constructed. Semioticians claim that news programs are metonymic in structure. (Metonymy is a figure of speech in which one word or phrase stands for another. The first word often consists of a condensed representation of the other word or phrase, such as the use of the word *Washington* to stand for the *United States government*.) Separate items are presented as "the news," with the suggestion that somehow they provide the composite knowledge required of the events of that day. In addition, a simple image is created to represent a complex issue.

One final aspect of the construction of news is what psychologists call the "fundamental attribution error" in human thinking. That error involves attributing to individuals responsibility for causation rather than to larger, more abstract entities, such as the background or context in which an event occurs. Some media people argue, however, that most viewers can only understand abstractions when they are personalized (Chandler, 2005).

Ericson (1998) concludes, "There is a need to appreciate news for what it is, a form of literary fiction that provides valuable facts about the human condition. . . . The morality plays that result from how journalists visualize fact remain vital to the mentalities and sensibilities of modern society" (8).

The image that we build of the terrorist—or the enemy in the form of the supporter of a militant Islamic jihad—is created through words and images, virtually all of which reach us through mediated communication channels. Symbolic interactionism tells us that people try to achieve goals through interaction with other people. The experience that arises from this interaction is shaped by the meanings that arise from the use of symbols within the social group. Through word and image, we frame the situation so that the strips—the individual shots that we put in the frame—achieve meaning for the ongoing activities of life.

Herbert Blumer, influenced by George H. Mead and John Dewey, said that human beings might best be understood in relation to their environment. Blumer outlined three core principles that lead to conclusions about how a person's self is created and how the person is socialized within the surrounding community. The principle of *meaning* is central in human behavior and states that people act toward other people and things based on the meaning that they have given to the other people or things. The second basic principle is *language*. Language lets people negotiate meaning through symbols—

words, images, gestures, and sounds. Mead said that naming something gives it meaning, and we don't really know about something until it is named. Therefore, naming is the basis for human society and provides the extent of our knowledge. By engaging in speech acts with others (*symbolic interaction*) people identify meaning through naming and are able to engage in discourse. The third basic principle of symbolic interactionism is *thought*. Thought modifies a person's interpretation of symbols. Thought provides an evaluation of the symbols and consists of a mental conversation with one's self. Thought provides some flexibility in one's interaction with symbols.

Image construction is derived from the language we use, which is evident in the wording of our news stories. We launch "first strikes"; they launch "sneak missile attacks." Our men are "loyal"; their men are "blindly obedient." Our missiles cause "collateral damage"; their missiles cause "civilian casualties." Our planes "suffer a high rate of attrition"; their planes "are shot out of the sky" (see O'Shaughnessy, 1999).

In the Kosovo war, stereotyping through language construction contributed to the interpretation of the conflict through the language used. Graham (2005) says, "The Serb Soldiers [*sic*] were described as ill disciplined, paranoid and drunk, the Albanians as innocent and helpless. Every picture of an Albanian refugee, mass grave or even the mention of the word genocide acted as justification of the war to the public" (1).

Image construction is also derived from the framed picture we paint of the enemy. When the picture elements assume an appearance very different from the appearance that we associate with our own kind, it is not difficult to develop a portrait of a fearful enemy. We see a robe or military uniform instead of jeans, kaffiyeh scarves to conceal the identities of the perpetrators, a swarthy, weather-beaten face, a Kalashnikov rifle on the hip, a phalanx of hooded men with rifles and swords lined up behind a kneeling hostage, a face of a known terrorist leader smiling cunningly in front of a wall of barren rock as he issues the latest threat to the West.

These characteristics of a pictorial image are viewed and interpreted in accordance with Morris's description of the function of signs. The *designative* aspect of signs directs the interpreter to specific objects or meaning elements. The sign designates something. The *appraisive* aspect of a sign orients the interpreter to the unique qualities of the denoted object. The interpreter evaluates the object. The *prescriptive* aspect directs the viewer to respond in certain ways. These ways are in harmony with the value and belief system that the viewer has internalized (Morris, 1946).

Therefore, the reality of the image of the terrorist is constructed socially and—intentionally or unintentionally—creates the face of fear that threatens the deep-seated elements of our beings, which we associate with our security and safety. That reality becomes a part of the way that we interpret the terrorist's argument and the way that we respond to that argument.

In conclusion, it would be instructive to recall Nietzsche's words, when he said, "Whoever fights monsters should see to it that in the process he does not become a monster. And when you look long into an abyss, the abyss also looks back into you" (Nietzsche, *Beyond Good and Evil*).

REFERENCES

Altheide, David L. 1997. The news media, the problem frame, and the production of fear. *The Sociological Quarterly*, 38, 4, 647-668.

Berger, Peter L. and Thomas Luckmann. 1966. *The social construction of reality: A treatise in the sociology of knowledge.* New York: Anchor Books.

Bernays, Edward L. 1929. *Crystallizing public opinion.* New York: Horace Liveright.

Boorstin, Daniel J. 1961. *The image: A guide to pseudo-events in America.* New York: Harper & Row.

Boulding, Kenneth E. 1956. *The image: Knowledge in life and society.* Ann Arbor, MI: The University of Michigan Press.

Chandler, Daniel. 2005. Notes on the construction of reality in tv news programs, June 15. Accessed December 29, 2005, from file://G:\The Construction of Reality in TV News Programmes.htm.

Croteau, David and William Hoynes. 2003. *Media society: Industries, images, and audiences* (3rd ed.). Thousand Oaks, CA: Pine Forge Press.

Ericson, Richard V. 1998. How journalists visualize facts. *Annals of the American Academy of Political & Social Science,* November, 560, 83-96. Accessed December 29, 2005, from Academic Search Elite, 1-11. http://www.unm.edu/~gassaway/visualizingfact.htm.

Ezrahi, Yaron. 2005. In Thomas L. Friedman, *The world is flat: A brief history of the twenty-first century.* New York: Farrar, Straus & Giroux.

Fiske, John. 1987. *Television culture.* London: Routledge.

Friedman, Thomas L. 2005. *The world is flat: A brief history of the twenty-first century.* New York: Farrar, Straus & Giroux.

Graham, James. 2005. Social construction of political realities via mass media in the Kosovo War. (Part Two), June 15. Accessed December 29, 2005, from file://G:\Social Construction in the Kosovo War Part 2.httm, 6/15/2005.

Keen, Sam. 1986. *Faces of the enemy: Reflections of the hostile imagination.* San Francisco: Harper & Row.

Lang, Kurt, and Gladys E. Lang. 2000. How Americans view the world: Media images and public knowledge. In *Media power, professionals and policies,* ed. Howard Tumber, 295-313. New York: Routledge.

Langer, Susanne K. 1957. *Philosophy in a new key: A Study in the symbolism of reason, rite, and art,* 3rd ed. Cambridge, MA: Harvard University Press.

Lewis, Justin. 1991. *The ideological octopus: An exploration of television and its audience.* London: Routledge.

Lippmann, Walter. 1922. *Public opinion.* New York: The Free Press.

Littlejohn, Stephen W. 2002. *Theories of human communication,*7th ed. Belmont, CA:Wadsworth.

Merskin, Debra. 2004. The construction of Arabs as enemies: Post-September 11 discourse of George W. Bush. *Mass Communication & Society,* 7, 2, 157-175.

McLuhan, Marshall. 1964. *Understanding media: The extensions of man.* New York: McGraw-Hill.

Morris, Charles W. 1946. *Signs, language, and behavior.* New York: Braziller.

McQuail, Denis. 2000. *McQuail's mass communication theory,* 4th ed. London: Sage.

——. 1987. *Mass communication theory: An introduction,* 2nd ed. London: Sage.

Nietzsche, Friedrich W. 1886. *Beyond good and evil: Prelude to a philosophy of the future.* Trans. Helen Zimmern. New York: 1907 Document: Book Libraries Worldwide, 12 (WorldCat).

NIH (National Institutes of Health) News. *Electrical impulses foster insulation of brain cells, speeding communications.* Accessed January 11, 2009, from http://www.nih.gov/news/pr/mar2006/nichd-17.htm.

O'Shaughnessy, Michael. 1999. *Media and society: An introduction.* South Melbourne, Australia: Oxford University Press.

Picard, Robert G. 1993. *Media portrayals of terrorism: Functions and meaning of news Coverage.* Ames, IA: Iowa State University Press.

Schutz, Afred. 1967. *The phenomenology of the social world.* Evanston, IL: Northwestern University Press.

——. 1970. *On phenomenology and social relations.* Chicago: University of Chicago Press.

Social construction. 2006. In *Wikipedia,* 1. Accessed July 10, 2006, from http://en.wikipedia.org/wiki/Social_construction.

Spillman, Kurt R., and Kati Spillman. 1997. Some sociobiological and psychological aspects of "Images of the Enemy." In Ragnhild Fisbig von Has and Ursula. Lehmkuhl, eds. *Enemy images in American history,* 43-64. Providence, RI: Berghan.

Van Zoonan, Elisabeth, A. 1992. The women's movement and the media: Constructing a public identity. *European Journal of Communication,* 7, 4, 453-476.

Wiener, Philip, P. ed. 1958. *Charles S. Peirce: Selected writings.* New York: Dover.

Chapter Four

Media Imagery:
Generator of Oppositional Schemas
That Fuel World Conflict

In Shakespeare's *Hamlet*, Rosencrantz, Guildenstern, and Hamlet argue briefly about the merits of living in Denmark. The debate centers on the contrasting ideas that Denmark is nearly a paradise and, conversely, that it is a prison. Hamlet dismisses the argument out of hand by saying, "There is nothing either good or bad, but thinking makes it so" (*Hamlet*, Act II, Sc. II).

The power of the mind to generate its own perception of reality is an ancient idea that has been shaped into the more modern form of the social construction of reality. Various authors have noted the significance of social interaction in molding the perception that we have of ourselves (e.g., Wilson, 2002; Berger and Luckman, 1966; Entman, 2004; Hassin, Uleman and Bargh, 2005; Reese, Gandy and Grant, 2003; Goffman, 1974). This sense of self is shaped by the language we use, the type of education to which we are exposed, and the norms and values that we learn at home, among our peers, as part of teams, in school, at work, at church, and within our social groups. Social constructivism suggests that our sense of identity and individuality is shaped largely through our reactions to other people.

This chapter examines the deep belief structures of society and suggests that once core values are internalized, they become a part of the unconscious mind that releases a particular value in response to some stimulus from a conflicting set of core values from an opposing society. The societies considered here are Islam and Christianity, National Socialism (Nazism) and Western democracy, and Soviet values as reflected in its propaganda against fascism and capitalism.

An assumption in this chapter is that the core values of a society become firmly entrenched as idea and affect fragments in the adaptive unconscious that provide a pattern that can spring to the fore in a knee-jerk reaction as a defense of one's own cherished values, or work their way into the conscious mind as a fleshed out form that can allow for a filling in of data for logical consideration.

In most cases, one's reaction to a stimulus from an opposing society—through the text of a news story, a picture, or a piece of propaganda—will induce an instantaneous wall of rejection of the unfriendly message, supported by intense emotion, such as hatred, contempt, or disgust. That response springs forth from the unconscious mind in its abbreviated (patterned) form to allow for a speedy defense of an attack so that the mind can return to a state of homeostasis. All of these functions involve use of the unconscious mind. All involve the coding of messages from the perspective of one's learned and internalized value system.

This author suggests that the core values reside in the adaptive unconscious and can be considered with related concepts such as schemas, typifications, stereotyping, profiling, and framing. In all of these cases, one is concerned with idea and emotion elements that, when activated, allow the mind to defend its belief foundation for a quick return to normalcy and without the necessity of elaboration of thought through logical analysis. This is what makes the core values such a powerful weapon in the war of values.

All of these functions are not identical, but they are cut out of the same cloth. They are all concerned with memory packets stored in the unconscious and brought to the fore in a form that assumes the hue and perspective of the value system that one is taught. All of these ideas and impulses are from one's own cultural perspective. This, by definition, sets them apart from schemas that arise from different cultures and different societal organizational patterns. Therefore, the stage is set for conflict.

THE SOCIAL CONSTRUCTION OF
REALITY IN DEVELOPING OPPOSITIONAL SCHEMAS

The social construction of reality is reflected in the construction of journalistic news stories. The communication practices of journalists—intentionally or unintentionally—shape facts into ways that they are perceived. Several observers suggest that there is a bias toward dominant or consensual values. That bias is derived from schemas that people build up in their lives through their interaction with members of their own societal groups and members of their own culture. *A schema is a pattern imposed on complex reality or experience to assist in explaining it, mediating perception, or guiding response.* Both schemas and framing are concerned with condensed packets of information, charged with emotion, that guide our conscious thought and direct our behavior.

Fredin (2003) links the concept of framing with that of a schema when he says that *people frame their experience in packets of information that are organized into patterns, stored in memory, and can be retrieved at will from memory.* In many respects, these frames are similar to news frames.

Entman (2004) describes framing as "the process of selecting and highlighting some aspects of a perceived reality, and enhancing the salience of an interpretation and evaluation of that reality" (26). Frames are persuasive mechanisms that actively direct thought, image, value, and affect in a particular direction. Such movement of thought includes interpretation of an event with a consequent evaluation and behavioral response. Fredin (2003) says, "Schemas function as efficient ways to quickly interpret events in daily life. In this regard, they are structures of expectation" (270).

THE ADAPTIVE UNCONSCIOUS AS
THE RESERVOIR OF VALUE CONFLICT

Psychology suggests that the adaptive unconscious is part of the architecture of the mind that is not accessible to conscious awareness. Just as people aren't able to observe how their kidneys work, people also aren't able to observe how they unconsciously categorize their environments, set goals, and generate intuition (Wilson, 2002, 18). The adaptive unconscious differs considerably from Sigmund Freud's concept of the unconscious, which was a chamber filled with desires and fantasies that had to be suppressed because they were incompatible with societal norms or because they couldn't be realized in conscious awareness. Gladwell (2005) suggests that the adaptive unconscious is a kind of giant computer that quickly and quietly processes a lot of the data we need in order to keep functioning as human beings.

The adaptive unconscious elevates process over internal turmoil. It might be thought of as a computer that processes streams of data that we need to function as organisms that occupy a particular environment. If we step into the intersection of a street and see a car heading directly in our direction, we respond very quickly to take evasive action. This is a process that can't be played out in response to conscious, logical analysis. There is no time for that. Action must depend on an automatic response based on data being fired into the decision-making portion of the brain from patterns derived from learning and experience. We make quick, predetermined judgments based on a small amount of information.

This process not only allows us to respond to imminent danger, but it also causes us to make snap judgments about people and situations. That suggests that the morally neutral action taken to avoid a speeding car bearing down on us is related to what might be either a moral or immoral act that arises from a stereotype. *A stereotype provides a fixed, unvarying form to something.* It is a conventional, formulaic, and oversimplified conception, opinion, or image—something that is regarded as embodying or conforming to a set image of type. Interestingly, the characteristics of a stereotype resemble very closely the characteristics of a typification. Typification refers to something that is represented by an image, a form, or a model. A typification embodies the essential characteristics of something, such as a painting that typifies an artist's work. A typification represents something through an image, a form, or a model. Thus, a typification embodies the essential patterned elements of an idea, an image, or an affect. The definition of "typification" or "stereotype" suggests that only a portion of the data associated with the whole concept resides in the memory packet in the unconscious mind. An example is only a representative portion of the broader concept that it is intended to illustrate. A model is an abbreviated portion of the thing that it represents. It has just enough object information to allow a picture of the whole to snap into place when the mind fills in the missing data. A "form" refers to an object that contains the essential information that would allow the mind to fill in the details so that the entire object assumes a complete high resolution image once the mind has filled in the missing data. A form refers to the essential nature of a thing as opposed to its matter.

The snap judgments that we make about people, situations, or things arise from a similarly patterned set of orientations based on our attitudes, opinions, beliefs, and values. The snap judgment that one might make about a different race is fired by a reservoir of unconscious beliefs that sends a vectored impulse into our conscious mind. We seem to be dealing with the same process in the adaptive unconscious, schemas, and stereotypes. The process may have positive, neutral, or negative social consequences.

Profiling also suggests the process by which data are accumulated, placed in patterns, and then analyzed for meaning. *A profile is a formal summary or analysis of data, often in the form of a graph or table, representing distinctive features or characteristics.* Once again, it is the truncation of data into economical patterns that store only the key elements of meaning in the unconscious recesses of the mind that represents the essence of profiling. In profiling, data are extracted from a pool of information of like ideas, impressions, and emotions that represent distinctive features or characteristics, flashed onto the screen of the mind in summarized form, and analyzed for meaning. The automatic filling in of detail from a simplified mosaic, with a skeletal outline but no flesh at first, is a process that seems to be characteristic of all of the categories of data retrieval associated with schemas, typifications. stereotypes, framing, and profiling. The adaptive unconscious is the apparent source of the information for all of these processes.

Wilson (2002) suggests that people's judgments and interpretations are generally guided by a desire to view the world in a way that gives them maximum pleasure—what he calls the "feel-good" criterion (38). The desire to feel good is probably universal and seems to be achieved with nonconscious thought. The things that make us feel good, however, depend on our culture, our personalities, and our level of self-esteem.

The adaptive unconscious actively processes information, which it first learns. It selects data, interprets them, evaluates them, and sets goals based on the data. Without that adaptive process, the level of human activity would be vastly reduced. However, this process should not be viewed as governed by some absolute standard of accuracy or moral rectitude. The adaptive unconscious is morally neutral. It is characterized by its ability to categorize objects and people in a moment; it fills in the blanks when we receive ambiguous information, much as we fill in the blank spaces of a mosaic when we view the object from an increasing distance.

This stereotyped impression that we get from such unconscious processing of information may have either positive or negative social effects. Therefore, the negative image and hateful feeling that we generate when we think of race or lifestyles is generally considered to be socially destructive. The point is that when we deal with the adaptive unconscious, we are dealing with an amorphous mass of values, attitudes, opinions and beliefs that are in a constant state of flux, taking one shape at this moment and slowly morphing into a different shape as varied life experiences are encountered. The same value sets respond to myriads of value-laden stimuli that we receive as messages that impinge on our brain. That is what makes us opinionated. The fact that we receive so many opinion-charged messages that are inconsistent with our own sets of opinions is the reason that it doesn't take long to determine a person's value system in a casual conversation on almost any subject.

It is, however, these value systems that are tapped when news reporters choose one word, as opposed to another, to paint a picture of an event, or choose one frame, as opposed to another, to provide one meaning to a picture, as opposed to another. When we paint a picture of an enemy through words and images on paper or a screen, we do so by creating a dichotomous image. The dichotomous image is created verbally by use of words such as "we" versus "they." Coloring in of the negative image occurs through references to "evil," "an evil empire," "demons," or, derisively, "those people."

A government uses the idea of a common enemy as a method of social control, a method of reinforcing the political, economic, and cultural values of the nation and as a mechanism for reinforcing those beliefs (see Keen, 1986; Spillman and Spillman, 1997). But, framing a message to direct attention and interest to one set of values—as opposed to another—may occur consciously (by persuader design) or unconsciously (by the communicator's unconscious choice of word and image that reflects his own value system).

Three steps are involved in the transition from the social construction of our sense of self and sense of community, the framed screen images and sounds that shape a portion of our reality, and the assessment of our reality through our adaptive unconscious. The unconscious assessment of our reality is dependent upon the character of those memory packets in the brain that store our codified beliefs, values, and impressions of the way the world is and the way that it should be. Those differences in the value and belief nodes are quite impervious to change and provide a ready source of stereotyped responses that arise from our adaptive unconscious. The carefully crafted design of our belief and value system generates powerful images—reinforced by powerful emotion—that place one set of societal values against another. The sharp contrast of belief systems sets the stage for the confrontation of worldviews. The seething and surging subsurface belief and value systems— only slowly changing, if at all—seem to create a climate for a struggle of cultures into the distant future. The media play an extremely important part in the transmission of images that energize the conflicting systems.

Even though our understanding of the adaptive unconscious, schemas, and stereotypes is far from complete, it seems reasonable to conclude that the deep-set value and belief system of the individual and the collectivity of individuals that make up a society function from the adaptive unconscious and surge forth as defense and reinforcement mechanisms when challenged by opposing systems. Because these oppositional mind-sets are stubborn, instantaneous, and resistant to change, they serve as powerful reinforcers of the status quo and barriers to thrusts from oppositional value and belief systems.

Entman (2004) distinguishes schemas from frames by saying that *schemas refer to interpretive processes that occur in the mind. Schemas are clusters of connected ideas and feelings stored in memory.* These clusters are psychological neighbors (and, perhaps, physiological neighbors as well). These psychological clusters are likely to be associated with each other.

Stereotypes seem to represent this same type of thought and *spring to the fore of conscious thought to reinforce a belief and, often, to reduce dissonance that arises when an event occurs that runs counter to the value and belief mind-set that is made up of a cognitive and affective charge that is stored in the unconscious.* Wilson (2002) says that an interesting property of the adaptive unconscious is that it uses stereotypes to categorize and evaluate other people. It is significant that schemas and stereotypes include an emotional charge that empowers the cognitive component of the schema or stereotype.

Entman (2004) notes the potential power of schemas when he says that habitual schemas are often organized into an overarching paradigm, or a meta-schema. Paradigms are networks of habitual schemas. These networks feed our analysis of news stories by causing us to draw analogies between our impression of the world and the cognitive and affective components of the news event that we are experiencing visually on a screen or text on a page or screen. This analogical association occurs as a result of priming, that is, activating an association between an item designated in the framed text and the viewer's thinking about a related concept. In the world of practical journalism, most news organizations minimize empathic images of enemy nations, thus reflecting and reinforcing Americans' lack of emotional connection with foreigners.

The adaptive unconscious is usually thought of as an evolutionary adaptation. As Wilson (2002) says, "the ability to size up our environments, disambiguate them, interpret them and initiate behavior quickly and nonconsciously confers a survival advantage and thus was selected for" (23). The adaptive unconscious plays a major role in our mental lives. It collects information, interprets and evaluates that information, and sets goals in motion. All of these steps are performed quickly and efficiently—almost instantaneously.

Stereotyping, also, has its organizational base in the adaptive unconscious. The characteristics of stereotyping seem to resemble other constructs that lie in the adaptive unconscious.

The first characteristic of the process of stereotyping is *simplification*. Idea and emotion are reduced to a skeletal minimum. Minimization of detail increases the processing speed substantially. Survival often requires blinding speed in decision-making.

A second characteristic of a stereotype is some sort of *exaggeration*. An exaggerated mental construct provides a definitive answer to what may be a thought with intertwined levels of complexity and uncertainty. The exaggerated thought eliminates dissonance and, thus, allows for a return to homeostasis.

A third characteristic of a stereotype involves *generalization*. Generalization involves minimizing detail. This, again, is a factor of speed. The less detail that one has to deal with, the faster one can dispose of a problem. The pointillistic omission of detail allows the mind to fill in missing data automatically and unconsciously.

The fourth characteristic of a stereotype is that it creates the impression that one's own *cultural attributes* are *natural*. This perception allows one to feel integrated with the idea structures of one's immediate environment. A sense of feeling at one with nature contributes to the powerful drive to achieve homeostasis.

The world of virtual reality created by images on a screen (photographic or textual) feeds from, reinforces, and contributes to our battery of stereotypical imagery. Stereotypical responses operate constantly. When we meet a person for the first time, we categorize the person according to our perceptions of compatibility according to race or gender or age or body type. Wilson (2002) suggests that this process of automatic stereotyping is probably innate. He suggests that people are prewired to fit other people into categories. Wilson (2002) says, "No one is born with a specific stereotype about another group, but once we learn these stereotypes, usually from our immediate culture, we are inclined to apply them nonconsciously, unintentionally, uncontrollably, and effortlessly" (53).

The emotion-charged idea that springs from our unconscious minds provides a defense mechanism for us. It builds a wall around our conscious selves that is both protective as a shield and defensively aggressive as a counterattack. These defensive walls protect our cultural values, our political values, our economic values, and our religious values. This isn't to suggest that our value systems are impervious to change; just as a walled fortress, however, can be overrun, so can value systems be changed, sometimes by persuasion but more often by force. This is to suggest that conflicts between nations, or warring groups, are aggravated by the blindness that sets in when the airbag of the stereotype is deployed. The concurrent phrase that issues forth when the airbag is deployed is, "God is on our side," meaning that the group's value system's defense mechanism has sprung forth as a protective shield.

SOME COMPARISON OF
RELIGIOUS CORE VALUE SYSTEMS

It is helpful to compare both religious and secular values. Both types of values can be the substance of the protective value system that is deployed as a shield and as a sword, the attack that is intended to deflect the enemy thrust in the overall process of defense. As one compares religious values, one can see fundamental differences in the core beliefs of the several religious idea constructs.

Consider Christianity and Islam, for example. The religions are consistent in their claim that there is only one God. In addition, each religion accepts the idea that there is a single administrator of God's will on earth. Christianity assigns that role to Jesus; Islam assigns that role to Muhammad. From there, however, the religious idea constructs begin to diverge.

The concept of *love* in Christianity is expressed extensively through the Gospels. Such love extends to the unlovely. Islam describes a *care for man,* also found in Christianity and Judaism, but there is no explicit message of love, as found in the Gospels (Edgar, 2004).

Christianity believes that the only true path to salvation is through adherence to its beliefs. Islam accepts Christianity and Judaism as valuable faiths; however, Islam ranks these on a lower level than Islam. A Muslim obligation extends to Christians and Jews, but nobody else (*Encyclopaedia of the Orient,* 2007, October 1).

Christianity urges its adherents to live a moral life. Immoral uses of the body create roadblocks on the way to salvation. These include evil thoughts, murder, adultery, sexual immorality, theft, false testimony, slander, greed, malice, deceit, lewdness, envy, arrogance, and foolishness (Leitch, 2006).

Under Islamic belief, where Sharia law has been adopted, the role of women is specifically prescribed and diverges considerably from the expectations of Christianity. Islam emphasizes the importance of housekeeping for women, although it doesn't prohibit women from working. Sunni Islamic law allows husbands to divorce their wives through a public proclamation of their intent. The word *talag* (I divorce) must be said three times in public (*Sharia,* 2006, August 2, 5).

Strict Muslim law states that a believer may not marry, or remain married to, an unbeliever (of either sex). A dress code is prescribed. For men, the loins must be covered from knee to waist. Women must be fully covered. Neither men nor women are to be viewed as sexual objects. A husband may physically discipline disobedient wives. The first step consists of a verbal admonishment. The second step is to refrain from intimate relations. The third step is to hit the wife.

Sharia law condones the death penalty for homosexual acts, and death by stoning is the penalty for adultery. Conversion by Muslims to other religions is apostasy; the penalty for apostasy is death. No freedom of speech applies to matters such as criticism of the prophet Muhammad.

Such a set of theocratic principles is incompatible with the fundamental principles of democracy. As the religious steps are set forth, one can see a dichotomous clash between core values of Islam and core values of Christianity. Sharia faithfully reflects the dogmas and divine rules laid down by religion. It is stable and invariable and offers comfort in its absoluteness.

These fundamental values become schemas that recede into the adaptive unconscious. They provide the frame by which we view the world; they provide a concept of what is right and what constitutes an absolute good. The condensed, unconscious, affect-charged element that makes up our value-reflecting idea clusters in the unconscious produces instantaneous stereotypic responses to image and verbal stimuli.

Wilson (2002) notes that an interesting property of the adaptive unconscious is that it uses stereotypes to categorize and evaluate people. More than a century earlier, William Carpenter (1874) noted that people develop habitual "tendencies of thought" that are nonconscious. These thought patterns could lead to unconscious prejudices that are even more dangerous because we can't consciously guard against them.

Secular values, too, can be developed in societies and then instilled in value systems that are internalized and subsumed into the unconscious. At some place in the memory banks of the brain lie the stocks of social knowledge that allow us to make sense quickly of what goes on around us and then allow us to structure our actions accordingly. The existence of typifications in our memory banks allows us to classify objects and actions that we experience, through observation or narrative recitation (storytelling that passes cultural values from one generation to the next), and develop response patterns to them. This is an economy measure. It saves thought, time, and energy. In some societies, secular values outweigh religious values in significance. But, the process of knee-jerk springing forth of reinforcement and defense mechanisms to conscious levels as a rallying cry for the defense of the society is the same for religious as it is for secular values.

SECULAR VALUE CLASH: NAZISM VS. WESTERN DEMOCRACY

A good example of a clash of secular values occurred in the 1930s and 1940s, with the rise of Nazism in Germany. It is important to retain historical perspective and realize that the values of Nazism were developed by some of the best thinkers in Europe at the time. Judgment, in hindsight, is of no value in understanding the situation in the context of that time. Nazi Germany and the West were examples of extreme contrasts of value systems.

Collectivism became a deep secular value in Germany; *individualism* was its counterpart in the West. *Decision* based on *instinct and passion* became a deep secular value in Germany; *decision* based on *reason (supported by logic and evidence)* was the Western counterpart. A Nazi value embraced the idea that *war and conflict motivated a society to improve itself from within*, accompanied by a zero-sum philosophy; the *Western counterpart* suggested that *production,* accompanied by win-win trade, *would* further the growth of the society. The Nazi value system embraced authoritarianism; the West embraced *liberalism. Maximum liberty should exist* so that people could live lives by their own choice and direction, with the understanding that they would respect other individuals to do the same. The Nazi value system embraced *socialism*; the Western value system embraced capitalism, where individual producers and consumers would decide for themselves (see Hicks, 2006).

The *National Socialists* (Nazis) were *visionary crusaders*. Inspired by Nietzsche's concept of the *Übermensch* (a refined, evolved form of a human being), the Nazis were not content to let man be what he is, at any given time period, but to give a push to further his evolutionary development. As crusaders, the Nazis were trying to improve the quality of the world.

Under *collectivism*, as opposed to Western *liberal individualism*, work should be an integral part of the life of all members of a society. Every individual must perform mental or physical work. Individuals should work for the community out of a sense of duty, not life, liberty, and the pursuit of happiness.

National Socialist values emphasized that individuals should *subordinate their personal lives* in favor of the *general welfare* of the community. The common interest takes precedence over self-interest. As socialism is endorsed, capitalism, in equal degree, must be replaced.

A key *value of the National Socialists*, which astounds people living in a capitalistic world today, involved the *abolition of all income gained by lending money at interest*. To be legitimate, money must arise from one's own effort, physical or mental, not through the charging of interest or usury.

Nazi belief encouraged the *confiscation of all profits earned by German business during World War I*. The German playing field needed to be leveled so that the new German industrial pattern could benefit from illegal profit made previously. The *new order* would involve the *nationalization* of all corporations. Profit sharing would be an integral part of large industrial enterprises.

The development of a strong *welfare state* became a deep-set value, with the generous development of state-run old age insurance. *Nationalization* included immediate *socialization* of large department stores.

Joseph Goebbels (see Hicks, 2006) verbalized some of the Nazi values with intellectual acuity and forthright statement. Goebbels berated capitalistic society in which a worker becomes a cog in a machine. The worker is alienated from what he produces. Racial and ethnic group identification is important because it gives nations their core identities.

Even though Marxism embraced collectivization, it was too narrowly focused on economic systems. Nazism rejects cosmopolitanism. Differentiation among groups should be based on ethnic characteristics and values.

The three central themes of National Socialism were *collectivism, socialism*, and *nationalization. Authoritarianism* and *centralized power* were favored as the engine to drive the political, economic, and social systems. *Racial identity* and *purification* were *necessary* to retain a unified focus on a nation's goals. The Nazi concept of sacrificing oneself for the greater good had overtones of the Christian value of altruism, but it was drawn with harsher psychological brush strokes.

Education had a *high priority* under National Socialism, and it emphasized the *coordinated development of mind and body.* Incidentally, the largest segment of the middle class in Nazi Germany consisted of elementary school teachers. Charles Darwin's concept of the survival of the fittest was reflected in the Nazi endorsement of eugenics, the natural selection of the strong through controlled selective breeding. All aspects of life were under state direction, not just monetary concerns, but also the biological interests of the state (see Hicks, 2006).

It is immediately evident that the core values depicted here are diametrically opposed to the core values of capitalism. The point, however, is that from whichever set of values one's perspective originates, the values are of equal depth and are subsumed into the adaptive unconscious in the same way. An image in a photo, a song, words in a newspaper article, an image on a TV screen or a computer screen will trigger the surfacing of a defensive typification. That image reflects a stereotype. To the extent that that image reflects one's cultural values, a wall is erected between this set of cultural values and others. The cultural reinforcement and defense mechanisms have taken over. One set of values is now pitted against the other. Because the points of departure are at extreme ends of a core value continuum, peaceful resolution is unlikely. Compromise is virtually impossible for polar opposite ideas. Only complete submission of one party by the other through physical force will create a vacuum whereby one set of values may replace the other. This occurred through the defeat of Germany in the Second World War and, to a slightly lesser extent, through the defeat of Japan during that same conflict.

When persuasion works, it usually works through the subtle displacement of one value by an equally subtle intrusion of a conflicting value. For example, during the Cold War, some residents of East Germany were exposed to the development of shopping facilities in the West. Stories brought back to East Germans whetted their appetite for shopping centers and abundant consumer goods. Today, in Minsk, Belarus, hardly a bastion of capitalistic values, a three-level shopping center has been developed in the subway station under Independence Square. Some of these stores are privately operated. This is hardly an indicator of major value change, but it does represent the way in which persuasion can intrude into a value system, offering the potential of seeping changes in at least portions of a value system. Where persuasion can be successful in value change, it must be through the introduction of aspects of another culture that are sought by the first culture and that they can accept willingly and peacefully. The shopping malls in West Germany during the Cold War intrigued the people of the East. The new mall in the subway in Minsk may represent a step in the liberalization of the value system of the Belarusians.

It is hard for people living under twenty-first century capitalism to grasp the profundity of some of the diametric value opposites. That the concept of earning money through the charging of interest would be considered anathema seems incredible to members of a capitalist society. Yet, the concept underlying that National Socialist value was that transference of money from one person to another should result in some positive production of goods or services. Money should stimulate production directly.

To the extent that core values such as these become part of the stored unconscious value packets in the brain, one can begin to get a sense of the affect-infused image that would arise in response to a related stimulus. An image from a propaganda poster, a phrase used in a news story, an image from a still photograph or a moving visual image would generate one typified response in a society that incorporated that concept, yet an opposite typified response in a society that has not incorporated such a concept. A typification that falls outside of a person's field of acceptable affect-infused images arises as an enemy and, therefore, deserves to be shunned or engaged defensively.

The words that are typically cited as personifying the diametrically opposite poles of the early twenty-first century between Islam and the West are "terrorist" and "freedom fighter." The word "terrorist" is used almost exclusively for people who use violence or who orchestrate violent behavior against the typifications that represent Western core values. The term "freedom fighter" is used to refer to exactly the same people described by Westerners as "terrorists." The perspective from which Islamic jihadists generate an opposite affect-induced typification creates an image of a warrior promoting one's cause, defending one's rights, one's freedom, one's opportunity for economic development, one's culture. The concepts of "good" and "evil" reside in the two terms that refer to a single entity. With the responses to the terms arising from the core values firmly entrenched in the unconscious mind, the conditions for combat are established immediately.

Changes of the core values through persuasion are possible, but very difficult. More often than not, change comes only when one society destroys the other completely. Then, the victorious culture can impose a new order on the vanquished culture. The core values reflective of the victorious culture can then be imposed on the now defenseless peoples of the vanquished culture. As the new culture assumes dominance, the new generations of the vanquished culture come to adopt the core values of their new rulers.

It seems naive to assume that typifications that represent core values of a culture can be changed easily, such as through simple goodwill or an extension of superficial kindness. As noted, this author believes that core value change is possible through persuasion, but this chapter suggests that that outcome is difficult and rare.

JIHADIST LANGUAGE THAT TAPS INTO CORE VALUES

Language reflecting core values is rampant on the internet, not only with the suggestion that the enemy's military weapons be destroyed, but also that targets that are in defiance of the principles of Islamic jihadist core values are to be attacked. Not only should the jihadists destroy completely the aircraft carrier USS John F. Kennedy and 12 escort vessels, but should also blow up clubs for "naked women" around the base (World Wide Web, 2007, 29). An attack on the object of core values is implicit in this statement. The internet announcement said, "the anticipated number of pig casualties is 200-300" (World Wide Web, 2007, 29). The reality of the military objectives aside, some of the military objectives and the language used to describe them arise from the jihadist core values that have become embedded in the adaptive unconscious, as well as, perhaps, being considered at a conscious level subsequently.

The internet has provided an opportunity to disseminate opinions that reflect core values more widely and more individually than previously. The internet gives jihadists a tool for propaganda. It provides access to large audiences free from media filters or government censorship. Such dissemination of messages can also be carried out with relative anonymity. The internet can make a local cause global by uniting common interest cells around the world in a common cause.

The ease with which words, still pictures, sound, and video can be processed and disseminated constantly around the globe has created the amateur citizen journalist, but it has also created propagandists for almost any cause. The Islamic jihadist has become very active in using the miniaturized tools of the journalist to disseminate messages on a constant basis. For example, "Al-Qaeda now sends out regular 'news bulletins' with a masked man in a studio recounting events from the many fronts of *jihad,* whether in Iraq, Afghanistan, Chechnya or Palestine. *Jihadi* ticker-tape feeds provide running updates on the number of Americans killed (about ten times more than the Pentagon's death toll)" (World Wide Web, 2007, 29).

War images are not only shown, but cheers punctuate an event as they might at a football game. The blowing up of an American Humvee is accompanied by shouts of *Allahu Akbar!* (God is Great). These images appear on the internet a few minutes after the explosion takes place. Some of the war footage is developed into films with musical soundtracks of male choirs singing songs such as *Caravans of Martyrs* (World Wide Web, 2007, 29). A computer video game was released, called *Night of Bush Capturing.* Players would shoot at images of American soldiers and ex-President George W. Bush. It is also reported that jihadists have started to create "residents" in the virtual world of a Second Life.

The hand-held video camera has become a weapon alongside the AK 47 and the RPG rocket launcher. The media in this war have assumed the role of perpetual propagandist. A message on one jihadist's computer said, "Film everything; this is good advice for all mujahideen (holy warriors). Brothers, don't disdain photography. You should be aware that every frame you take is as good as a missile fired at the Crusader enemy and his puppets" (World Wide Web, 2007, 29).

A final point to be made about jihadi use of websites is that they are used heavily for indoctrination. Some Western intelligence experts consider this a greater danger than promotion of the war effort itself. Jihadi websites deal heavily with ideological and cultural questions, in which the values of the jihadist are brought to the fore. "At least 60 percent of the material on jihadi websites deals not with current events or war videos" (World Wide Web, 2007, 30). Rather, these websites deal with questions of values. A senior fellow at an American research institute suggests that jihadist material on the internet is less a war against the West than it is a war to win the minds of Muslim youth. Of course, the material could serve both objectives.

SOVIET PROPAGANDA AS A
REFLECTION *OF CORE VALUES*

Propaganda tends to focus on one of two themes. The first theme is intended to generate fear through depicting the enemy as a ruthless, vicious, predatory monster. The second theme belittles the enemy through caricature and ridicule.

Under Marxism/Leninism, for example, the Soviet Union used a grotesque caricature of the fat, evil, cigar-smoking capitalist glowering from a haughty arrogance generated by wealth and power. This theme about American imperialists had many variations, but the theme was consistent and uniform.

During World War II, Soviet propaganda focused on fascist barbarians. The monster enemy was to be confronted by heroic patriots of the motherland. Capitalists were also depicted as sharks. This propaganda capitalized on

Figure 4.1. A caricature takes a basic value and exaggerates the features of a character representing that value. The distortion of features simplifies the picture elements, making them easy to remember, and intensifies the emotion generated by an image that personifies a detested value. This photo depicts the greed and ruthless self-interest of the capitalist.

attack themes. A fourth theme was proactive and exalted cultural themes that promoted and reinforced Soviet Marxism/Leninism.

Soviet anti-American propaganda caricatured the capitalist, with fat jowls, scowling mouth, and eyes that rolled and bulged in their sockets. A sharp contrast was drawn between the evil and ruthless capitalist and the oppressed American, often depicted as blacks. One short propaganda film pictured blacks in electric chairs with the Negro spiritual, *Sometimes I Feel Like a Motherless Child,* playing in the background.

The contrast between opulent wealth and downtrodden poverty was depicted through background shots of skyscrapers and billboards showing products such as Cutty Sark whiskey and Camel cigarettes. In the foreground, a poorly dressed, bent-over black walked on a sidewalk in front of the billboards.

A contrast between the life of luxury lived by the capitalist and the oppression of the workingman was drawn in many Soviet propaganda messages. An occasional propaganda film would show the Soviets deftly frustrating a capitalist through sly trickery. In one of these films, an American imperialist, Mr. Twister, was depicted as racially prejudiced against blacks and Asians.

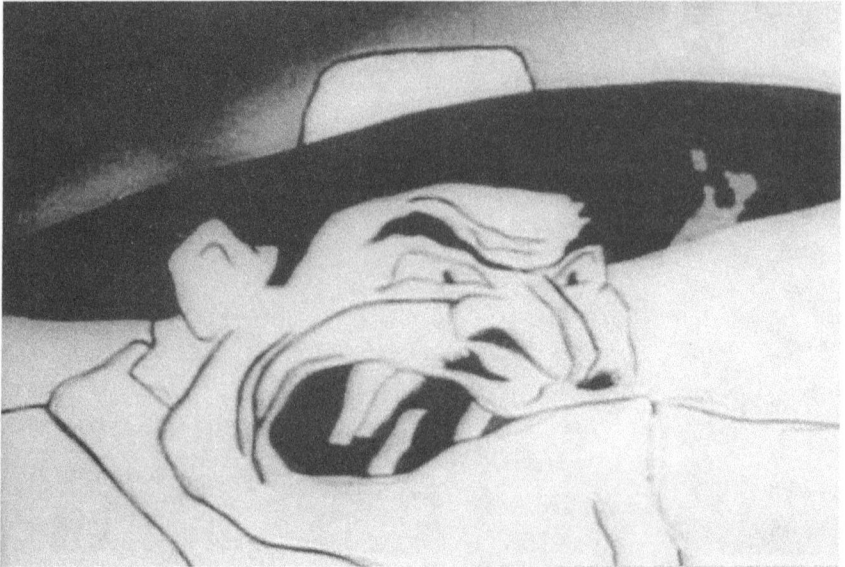

Figure 4.2. Wild as a carnivore bringing down its prey, the voracious capitalist is greedy, single-minded, and ruthless in his attempt to accumulate capital and power for himself. The frenzy of the capitalist in achieving his objectives at any cost is depicted in this photo. The ability of the artist to convey a powerful, multi-faceted idea with very few lines and depicting very few features is conveyed forcefully in this photographic drawing.

Mr. Twister checked in to a Moscow hotel and saw a black man coming down the stairs. He immediately returned to the front desk and checked out of the hotel. To thwart Mr. Twister, the concierge called all of the other hotels in the city and urged them to refuse lodging to Mr. Twister, thus providing a uniform blackmail of the evil capitalist. Mr. Twister went from hotel to hotel, only to find no vacancy signs wherever he went. Mr. Twister then dreamed that he had flown back to sympathetic America and had sought a hotel room there, only to be confronted by the same *no rooms available* sign that he had experienced in Moscow (*Animated Soviet Propaganda*, 2006).

During the Cold War, a *grass is always greener* theme underlay some of the propaganda films. The obvious intent of this theme was to discourage Soviet citizens from thinking that life might be better in the West. Jazz music was often used as a symbol of the decadent West (America in particular).

The vast majority of propaganda messages used caricature, ridicule, and sarcasm to depict the enemy. A few themes, intended for local consumption, glorified the values and goals of the state. Propaganda, of course, was directed not only at the enemy (and the picture that one wanted to create of

Figure 4.3. Hitler is caricatured as a horned pig. Just enough characteristics of Hitler are drawn into this caricature so that it takes a moment or two for the mind to fill in the missing picture elements and to identify Hitler as the object and associate it with a pig.

the enemy), but also it served as a proactive tool to reinforce existing beliefs in the values of the society and the objectives of the state.

Whereas the Soviet propaganda image depicted the American capitalist as an evil-eyed, fat-jowled, self-centered, cigar-smoking controller, the picture painted of the fascist was quite different. The fascists were depicted as long-snouted hungry pigs in horned helmets. Hitler was depicted as a fat slob training a group of dogs to be blindly obedient.

In an ironic twist, one short film showed Hitler visiting the tomb of Napoleon and asking Napoleon for his blessing to conquer the world. Napoleon muttered agreement from his tomb and then extended a distorted, skeletal arm for Hitler to shake. Hitler recoiled from the bony hand in terror. He turned to run, but the skeletal hand seized the back of Hitler's coat. Circus music played underneath, lending a satirical emphasis to the visual image.

In addition to ridiculing the fascists, a number of the Soviet efforts were resistance films, which urged the Red army and all Soviet citizens to resist the fascist incursion into their homeland. One theme declared that the Red army would not allow the enemy to conquer our homeland. We will drive the invaders from our land. Vultures, with swastikas painted on them flew overhead and then morphed into fighter-bombers that rained down a hail of bombs. Aerial dogfights showed Russian fighters shooting down German planes.

Figure 4.4. The ravenous, Nazi, horned pig strikes out beyond his own territory in search of lands to conquer and people to subdue and enslave. The determination and intent of the intruder are depicted in this caricature, which suggests lightning speed into neighboring territories and a focused will with a disregard for potential victims.

The idea in most of these propaganda pieces was implicit in the image; however, ideas were occasionally dealt with through logical reasoning regarding the conflict between core values or political objectives. Some Soviet propaganda pieces combined verbal argument and imagery to depict the objectives of the fascists. One argument claimed that Hitler wanted the land of the Soviet Union for his gain. The argument went as follows: Hitler wants to steal grain from our communal farmers. Hitler wants our industry to turn over to capitalists. He wants land to turn over to landlords. Hitler wants to enslave our free people.

One image showed Hitler riding on the back of a bent-over laborer, who had his hands tied behind his back. At times, a threat element was introduced into the propaganda: that Hitler would get three blows for each one that he delivers; that Hitler would get ten fires for each fire he starts; that Hitler would get the bayonet, the rifle, hot lead. Hitler would see fascism's inglorious end. On that note, Hitler is shown slumped over with a scythe through his heart.

Domestic propaganda in the United States frequently had an economic theme and urged people who couldn't enlist to invest in the economy by buying Liberty Bonds (later referred to as Victory Bonds, then Savings Bonds,

Figure 4.5. In Figure 4.5 and Figure 4.6, the vulture value of Nazism is depicted in morphed, metaphorical images. **Figure 4.5** depicts the value of the invader, the predatory bird that waits greedily for carrion. The swastika on the bellies of the birds associates clearly the character of the birds and the political system that they represent. The vultures are staining neighboring territories with their bloodthirsty onslaught.

and now Patriot Bonds). The primary objective of the Victory Bonds was not primarily to feed money into the war effort; rather, the purpose was to remove money from the economy in an effort to discourage inflation. To a lesser extent, Soviet domestic propaganda urged citizens to buy Liberty Bonds: *We'll beat them with our rubles.*

Dichotomous themes permeate much of Soviet propaganda. Positive proactive themes urged solidarity, strength, determination to resist the enemy, and a commitment to the values of Marxism/Leninism. The hallmarks of the pro-Soviet effort were the development of science, constant struggle, and toil. Citizens should take to the factories, the fields, the mines and pull together for the strength of the party and the strength to beat the enemy. The red flag of labor was raised high.

Persuasive ideas were also presented about capitalism. Installment buying and paying with credit were depicted as practices that would eventually destroy society. The constant interruption of television programming with blocks of advertising were seen as an affront to any artistic quality a television program might have. Advertising itself was portrayed as a kind of disinformation that makes outlandish promises that cause complete deception.

Figure 4.6. The figure of the vultures—morphed into warplanes—draws the metaphor between the vultures and the bombers in compelling imagery. The link between
the character and the intent of the enemy—the vultures—and the method of execution of that intent—the use of military might—is shown graphically in Figure 4.5 and
Figure 4.6.

But, the cold-hearted focus on capitalism as the bottom-line interest of
American society was depicted most trenchantly in a narrative about a mythical American corporation, the Pearson Company. This company was depicted
as having been passed from generation to generation and made anything that
would sell—guns, airplanes, bombs, and a cosmetic processor that turns every woman into a Miss America.

One employee, Michael Chase, rose to a high position in the management
structure of the company and became a shareholder. Because of the vagaries
of business, the Pearson Company unceremoniously eliminated Michael
Chase's position and he was summarily fired. The former manager then took
his place among other unemployed laborers, all wearing signs that said, *looking for work.*

The argument was then developed that installment and credit buying result
in misery, defeat, and destruction—first for the low class or middle class
individual forced to use installment and credit plans—but then for society
as a whole as foreclosures drive the population into desperation. Unemploy-
ment results in homelessness, turning to whiskey, and eventually, to forceful
restraint by police as desperation leads to violence.

Figure 4.7. An inspirational Soviet poster shows a strong, young woman, gazing upward, hopefully and expectantly, as the Soviet sword from the East and the British and American swords from the West cut the shackles of Nazi tyranny. The poster says, "Europe will be free."

As the society is decaying around the Pearson Company, the current Pearson Chief Executive Officer celebrates his dog's birthday. Michael Chase, meanwhile, has taken to driving stock cars for small amounts of cash. At one point, as Chase took the lead in a race, his car was bumped, spinning it out of control, resulting in a fiery crash, which left Chase seriously injured—all of this to the shouts of delight from the frenzied crowd.

The propaganda for domestic consumption in the Soviet Union emphasized the unification of the Soviet state under Marxism and the elimination of oppression from other states and religion that had bedeviled Russia prior to the 1917 revolution. The revolution decreed peace and promised a unified land. The builders of the new Communist state were pictured as strong, noble young men (and often women) shot mostly from a low camera angle. The existing promise of the new regime was depicted through heroic shots of young workers running or posing in exalted confidence.

ORIGIN OF THE CURRENT
CARICATURE OF THE IMPERIALIST

The caricature of the Western imperialist was created in graphic detail with the effort to breach the walls of the *Dragon Empire* in the late nineteenth century. For most of its 4,000-year history, China allowed very few Westerners into its closed society. Imperialists from several Western countries wanted to penetrate the *Yellow Wall* to expand their spheres of influence. This included Great Britain, France, Russia, and, after the Spanish American war of 1898, America, which was also interested in a physical presence in China.

The Chinese labeled these powers *foreign devils*, and, soon, the form of the imperialist predator appeared in caricature. Word and image, with a propagandist bent, were brought into play against the imperialists.

The first attack on China's internal structure was the smuggling of opium into China in the early nineteenth century. Opium was produced in India (then ruled by Great Britain) and smuggled into China, to the substantial financial benefit of the Western drug smugglers. By the 1840s, many Chinese were addicted to opium. The first attack, therefore, on Chinese society was, in effect, a physical commando strike designed to soften the underbelly of the enemy— the widespread distribution of a highly addictive drug into the society. It was also, of course, part of the imperialist capitalists' plan to acquire the resources of the *Dragon Empire* to enhance the wealth of their empires.

The *Yellow Wall*, however, remained impenetrable. Christian missionaries were proselytizing actively at this time, and the imperialists decided to enlist the missionaries to chip a hole in the wall, which could, subsequently, be

Figure 4.8. The imperialist attack on the rich, but closed, society of China began in the nineteenth century and continued into the early twentieth century. This caricature shows the imperial powers—Great Britain, France, Russia, and America—hovering over a young, Chinese peasant woman (representing Chinese society) as they prepare to devour her. A wealthy Chinese collaborator looks on.

opened for the insertion of military troops. The role of the missionaries constituted a form of psychological warfare. The Christians used their message of warmth, love, and "nonjudgmental" acceptance of any beliefs as an entrée into the religious structure of Chinese society. Christianity taught a value system that included *humility* (The fear of the Lord is a training in wisdom, and the way to honor is humility [Prov.15:33]); a passive acceptance of violence (You have learned that they were told, "Eye for eye, tooth for tooth." But . . . if someone slaps you on the right cheek, turn and offer him your left [Math.5:38-40]; and acceptance of the Other through an all-embracing love (love thy neighbor as thyself [Lev.19:18]). The principle of passivity and open acceptance of the Other was, in effect, the second imperialist step in breaching the *Yellow Wall*. Once inside the "walled" city, military action could further the interests of the imperialists directly. The Christian value system softened the will of the Chinese to resist their persecutors by force.

China's *closed door* policy was cracked open. China was forced to open more ports to trade and to cede adjacent territories to the West. England annexed Hong Kong and Kowloon to add to its existing Asian colonies. France took control of Indochina (Vietnam, Cambodia, and Laos). Russia assumed

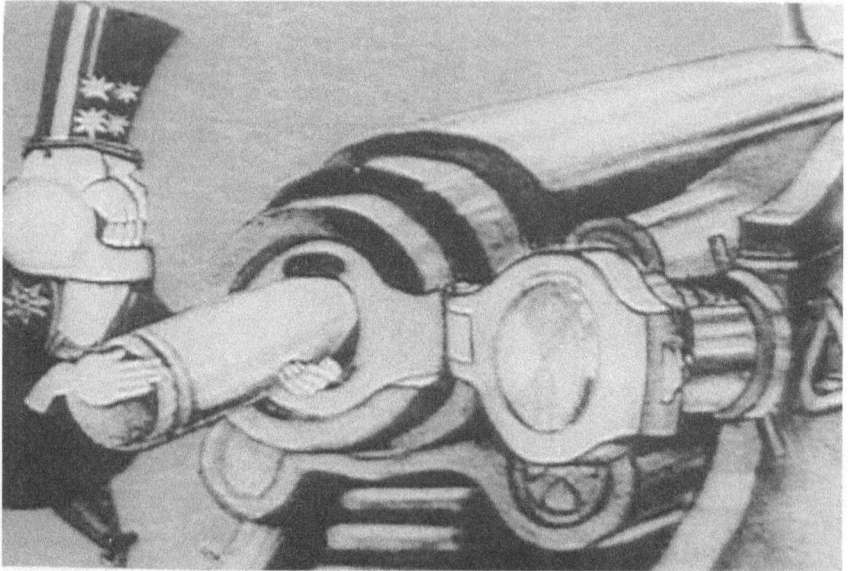

Figure 4.9. The imperialist mechanism for gaining control and dominating a society consisted primarily of the use of military force. America, in particular, was shown as trigger-happy and letting military might be the principle tool of "persuasion."

control of Chinese Turkestan and Manchuria. Japan seized Taiwan and won dominance over Korea. The United States, more interested in trade than in territory, negotiated The Open Door Policy in 1899 to ensure *equal and impartial* Chinese trade among Western imperialists. The Chinese people were humiliated and defensive. The Chinese launched a counterattack in the form of the *Boxer Rebellion* in 1900, but this military effort was squelched, and the Qing Dynasty (formerly Ch'ing Dynasty), established in 1644, fell in 1911 (see *The Eagle and the Dragon*).

The role of the Christian missionaries, in the struggle between the East and the West, gradually became understood by the Chinese who caricatured the missionary as an obsequious sycophant intent on carrying out the will of his imperialist masters.

PERSUASION, VALUES, AND
THE ADAPTIVE UNCONSCIOUS

Propaganda functions at two levels. The first level attempts to destroy the credibility of the enemy through ridicule. The caricature is an effective way to accomplish that objective. The second level pits the constructs of the core

Figure 4.10.   Christian missionaries, interested in proselytizing the populous country of China, were shown to be in collusion with the imperialists and appeared indifferent to their masters' use of guns and money to exercise their will. The missionaries functioned as an advance guard in the imperialist effort to breach the wall enclosing the society of China.

values of one society against the corresponding constructs of the opposing society

Language, image, and sound are shaped by our internalized cultural concepts that reside in the adaptive unconscious and leap to the surface to shape our oppositional images, words, and sounds that serve as protective shield and sword against the value-charged ideational concepts of the enemy. We are raising a defensive curtain around ourselves as an integral part of our collective society. Although the arguments may rise to the level of conscious thought and may be dealt with through progressive rational thought processes, most of the idea/image/affect seems to be processed at the unconscious level and serves to strengthen and sharpen our stereotypes.

The lines of a caricature provide just enough information to suggest the pattern of the image in the adaptive unconscious, much as a mosaic provides just enough picture information so that the mind fills in the missing data when the viewer achieves a certain distance from the mosaic. The incomplete picture elements of the mosaic suddenly assume the form of the image as the viewer's mind fills in the details of the missing picture elements. At that point, the image, the meaning associated with the image, and the emotional

Figure 4.11. The Christian missionaries had their own religious interest in Christian-izing Chinese society, but they weren't above accepting the support of the imperial-ists. The Chinese considered the missionaries part of the enemy intrusion into their society.

impact associated with the image converge in the conscious mind to create the artistic experience of that moment. The meaning of the details that are filled in are colored by the preconceptions of the associated category of data in the unconscious mind, namely the typifications and stereotypes making up the data pool in the unconscious mind.

Assuming that we have data sets in the unconscious mind for the core val-ues of our society—its political construct, its economic construct, its cultural construct—it is not surprising that the image of an appropriate, a correct idea of reality emerges when the associated idea packets in the unconscious mind are triggered by an image, a piece of text, or a piece of music. The associ-ated idea elements existing in the unconscious mind rush to consciousness to assume complete form (as the image of the mosaic becomes a picture when the appropriate distance from it is achieved). Once the typified image of a core value has sprung into consciousness, it assumes its position as an attack mechanism (a determined feeling of opposition to the enemy) and a defense mechanism (a welling up of determined resistance in support of one's value system).

Because the ideas and emotions that originate in very different (often dia-metrically opposed) core value systems assume shape as opposing warriors, it seems inevitable that these systems will clash in reality. Armed conflict, police actions, war will be the result if the opposing sides have weapons of war that can be used against the other—from armies, to suicide bombers, to information control for purposes of gaining a knowledge advantage over the enemy.

Core values, as with other societally shaped values (such as approach-and-avoid gradients to objects in our environment) seem to be learned socially and then internalized into packets of associated thought in the adaptive unconscious. It seems likely that the information packets contain the data in a condensed form (much as in the form of a mosaic) ready to be released as an airbag of protection when triggered by a crash involving conflicting ideas. These ideas arise containing not only idea, but also image, meaning, and affect. This is the reactive pattern of the stereotype. Speed is of the essence in translating the unconscious thought to a behavior (a defensive maneuver) that will cause one, reactively, to step back from a speeding car bearing down on a person, or a stereotype that will defend a cherished core value against the "speeding car" of an opposing value.

A stereotypical image of another person, another race, another gender, another lifestyle, or of elderly people, or of the young has as its purpose to throw up a defensive wall around us designed to protect the sensitive "inner organs" of our own belief systems. That defensive wall serves to bolster the individual's self-esteem. Therefore, typifications, stereotypes, and self-esteem work hand in glove to create an individual—and, collectively, a society—that has a phototropic bent toward a collective value system. When those entities clash, some sort of outcome is inevitable—armed conflict, avoidance through physical isolation, and, upon rare occasions, movement from one belief system to another through persuasion.

REFERENCES

Animated Soviet propaganda: From the October revolution to Perestroika. 2006. [Motion picture]. (Available from Films by Jove, http://www.russiananimation .com)

A world wide web of terror. 2007. *The Economist*, July 14, 29-30.

Berger, Peter L. and Thomas Luckmann. 1967. *The social construction of reality: A treatise in the sociology of knowledge.* New York: Anchor Books.

Carpenter, William B. 1874. *Principles of mental physiology.* New York: D. Appleton.

The Eagle and the Dragon. Accessed February 2, 2009, from http://hoover.archives .gov/exhibits/China/Political%20Evolution/index.html -18k.

Edgar, Brian. 2004. *Eight core Christian values.* Accessed November 22, 2007, from http://ea.org.au/election.

Encyclopaedia of the orient. 2007, October 1. Accessed November 22, 2007, from http://i-cias.com/e.o/is/am.htm.

Entman, Robert M.. 2004. *Projections of power: Framing news, public opinion, and U.S. foreign policy.* Chicago: The University of Chicago Press.

Fredin, Eric S. 2003. Frame breaking and creativity: A frame database for hypermedia news. In Stephen D. Reese, Oscar H. Gandy, Jr., and August. E. Grant, eds. *Framing public life: Perspectives on media and our understanding of the social world.* Mahway, NJ: Lawrence Erlbaum.

Gladwell, Malcolm. 2005. *Blink: The power of thinking without thinking.* New York: Little, Brown.

Goffman, Erving. 1974. *Frame analysis: An essay on the organization of experience.* Boston: Northeastern University Press.

Hassin, Ran R., James S. Uleman, and John A. Bargh, eds. 2005. *The new unconscious.* New York: Oxford University Press.

Hicks, Stephen. 2006. *Nietzsche and the Nazis* [Motion picture]. (Available from Ockham's Razor Publishing, http://www.ockhamsrazorpublishing.com)

Keen, Sam. 1986. *Faces of the enemy: Reflections of the hostile imagination.* San Francisco: Harper & Row.

Leitch, Cliff. 2006. *What the Bible says about Christian values and Christian living.* Accessed November 22, 2007, from http://www.TwoPaths.com. [Master Index].

Reese, Stephen D., Oscar H. Gandy, Jr., and August E. Grant, eds. 2003. *Framing public life: Perspectives on media and our understanding of the social world.* Mahway, NJ: Lawrence Erlbaum.

Sharia. 2006, August 2. Accessed November 22, 2007, from http://en.wikipedia.org/wiki/Sharia.

Spillman, Kurt R., and Kati Spillman. 1997. Some sociobiological and psychological aspects of "Images of the Enemy." In Ragnhild Fisbig von Has and Ursula Lehmkuhl, eds. *Enemy images in American history,* 43-64. Providence, RI: Berghan.

Wilson, Timothy D. 2002. *Strangers to ourselves: Discovering the adaptive unconscious.* Cambridge, MA: The Belknap Press of Harvard University Press.

Chapter Five

From the Seed to the Tree and Back Again: Definition of Linguistic Purpose

FROM ITS ORIGINS TO MODERN TIMES

Communication, fundamentally, involves the transfer of idea, feeling, or image (which conveys an idea and associated feeling) from one responsive brain to another. The communication may be verbal, non-verbal, musical, or random noises. From the beginning of life forms, communication has guided the behavior of living beings and, under congenial environmental conditions, has allowed for the survival of a species.

HISTORICAL DEVELOPMENT OF THE STUDY OF COMMUNICATION

From the beginning, communication has involved a comprehensive mix of elements to convey a message—idea, feeling, picture, pleasure, or pain. That constant blend of purposeful, expressive elements makes communication a very complex subject.

Once mankind became aware of some of the elements of communication, an incipient formal study of the communication phenomenon led people to divide it into its several parts so that each facet of communication could be studied more effectively, that is, each part in isolation from the other. The purpose of the study in each case was to allow for a more accurate, precise, and powerful conveyance of idea and feeling (image is actually a way of conveying both idea and feeling powerfully) within the context of a given message.

The thesis of this chapter is that communication is a comprehensive activity that encapsulates all of the purposes of message transfer—information, persuasion, entertainment, and personal pleasure or pain. Although divisions of communication purpose may be useful in allowing for the determination of refined knowledge of the various arms of the communication activity, the pockets of information must, ultimately, be compressed in a unified whole in order to understand fully the purpose of communication and its function.

Aristotle (trans.1886) suggested the universality of communication when he said, "Rhetoric may be defined as a faculty of discovering all the possible means of persuasion in any subject. For this is exclusively the function of Rhetoric, as every other art, whether instructive or persuasive, deals with a subject-matter peculiar to itself . . ." (10).

Even though Aristotle recognizes divisions of purpose in communication, he also seems to recognize the interrelated nature of the activity—the universality of the communication process itself. Therefore, any consideration of either the art or science of communication—its logical, emotional, instructional, and pleasure components—should include the way that communication elements relate to a culture's core values and, generally, either project or reflect aspects of a particular culture.

The totality of meaning in words—in speech and in writing—gave them a magical power in ancient civilizations. Černý (1951) notes, "Speech . . . had a magic power [in ancient Egypt]: to pronounce words was to evoke in the supernatural world the things which they designated" (57). The fact that words were associated with things and gave the user of the word a total connectivity with the thing represented—idea, feeling, form, color—suggests that the word—and words in syntactic order—communicated a composite impression on the receiver of the word. Černý (1951) says, "Names, in particular, were closely connected with the substance of the thing or person named; the knowledge of their name gave one power over them: the god Ptah created the things of the visible world simply by naming them" (57-58). (See, for example, Plato's *Theory of Forms*.)

The magic of words in ancient Egypt resulted from the totality of the way that they conveyed meaning—idea (abstract and concrete), feeling, and form. The Egyptian hieroglyph was powerful not only because it conveyed idea, but also because it encapsulated that idea in an image, which extended the impact of the image not only as idea, but also as a thing in reality to which one can react with one's five senses—sight, sound, smell, taste, and touch. The word creates reality. Černý (1951) states the following:

> The hieroglyphs consisting of images of living beings and inanimate objects were more imbued with potential magic than any other kind of writing, since, in addition to the existence and power of the words they expressed, the individual figures of human beings and animals they represented were also capable of assuming a mysterious existence. (58)

As time went on, people began to inquire about the nature of the communication process and began to explore the character of the communication process itself and ways in which communication could be made more effective. As this process progressed, the components of communication began to be isolated, and attention was directed at one or another of the facets of communication to see how they worked and to examine ways of improving the quality of idea transmission to achieve more effectively the ends of communication—to allow for some sort of modification of human behavior.

An early effort to structure communication so that it would function more effectively at resolving the world's paradoxes was the development of dialectic as a mode of thought. Dialectic is a process of reasoning to reveal truth and obtain knowledge. The structure of dialectical reasoning split into diverging paths. Plato considered dialectic as a valuable vehicle to arrive at truth. Dialectic, Plato believed, is like dialogue and is closely associated with the Socratic method. Aristotle also considered the properties of dialectic but ranked it below rhetoric as a form of reasoning. Aristotle objected to dialectic because it was based on *a priori* knowledge rather than empirical observation. Cicero considered dialectic and rhetoric in much the same light as did Aristotle.

Interest in dialectic has continued in modern times, beginning with Kant and becoming an important part of German philosophy. Hegel introduced a specific structure for arriving at the truth. Hegel's three-step process was intended to improve the accuracy of resolution of the world's paradoxes. Hegel's three-step process starts with the formulation of a thesis, a static, clearly defined concept. From there, one structures an idea that is diametrically opposed to the thesis. This is the antithesis. The antithesis represents the ideas which are associated with the thesis but which seem to negate the corresponding elements of the thesis. Blending the knowledge components of the thesis and the antithesis allows for a new idea structure—the synthesis—which provides an advanced view of the contradictory aspects of the world and deepens mankind's understanding of the world. This process can be repeated indefinitely until knowledge and understanding gradually increase.

A sixth diverging path of dialectic involved Marx's dialectical materialism. Whereas Hegel's construction of dialectic was based on Idealism, Marx's construction was based on Materialism. Hegel assumed that rationality was the world's driving force; Marx assumed that material forces were the driving force of the world. Marx's dialectical materialism considers the contradiction among classes, the force of production, and the way that those forces interact.

The divergence of paths and the specialization of interest in communication began to detract attention from communication as a whole and began to set schools representing each discipline in opposition to one another. Although Aristotle recognized dialectic as a legitimate way to seek the truth and generate knowledge, Aristotle developed a new way of thinking about communication and developed a path that emphasized its persuasive nature. Aristotle said that dialectic was an effort to discover the real and apparent syllogism. Rhetoric was developed to discover the real or apparent means of persuasion. Dialectic and rhetoric are close cousins, but Aristotle defined rhetoric as a means of discovering all of the possible means of persuasion in any subject. Aristotle also extended the scope of rhetoric to all classes of subjects. The principles of rhetoric could be used by anyone who has a persuasive (or instructive) purpose. Aristotle (1886) said,

> Rhetoric on the other hand may be said to possess the faculty of discovering the means of persuasion in any given subject; and accordingly we hold that the rules of the rhetorical art are not limited in their application to a certain special definite class of subjects. (10)

The distinction between the word "instructive," as opposed to "persuasive," depends upon whether the arts are "exact" arts or "inexact" arts. (Aristotle, Weldon trans. 1886, (10). Rhetoric, then, incorporates principles from dialectic and ethics. Aristotle thus expands the scope of the study of speech communication. Cicero and Quintilian expanded the field of rhetoric some but in directions which Aristotle had ignored.

Rhetoric was formulated into a discipline that was part of both Roman and Greek cultures. During the Middle Ages, rhetoric was one of the subjects of the trivium. The other two subjects (in this lower division of the seven liberal arts in medieval schools) were grammar and logic. Incidentally, the upper division of the seven liberal arts—the quadrivium—consisted of geometry, astronomy, arithmetic, and music.

Since the revival of learning in the sixteenth and seventeenth centuries (through the Renaissance and the Enlightenment), rhetoric became a part of the university curriculum. As the development of the speech communication tradition approached the twentieth century, some students of speech emphasized its elocutionary aspects. The form of the expression itself—delivery, gesture, and vocal production—was studied as an important end objective of the speech process.

The four basic purposes of speech identified by McBurney and Wrage (1955) defined speech communication in the early- and mid-twentieth century. The speech purpose may be *inquiry, reporting, advocacy,* and *evocation.* Discussion is the typical form that is assumed when a speaker (within a group) is searching for information or insights.

Reporting involves conveying information, what is now generally referred to as informative speaking (or writing). The speaker's purpose is to convey information to one's listeners. Advocacy refers to what is now generally called persuasive speaking. The persuasive speaker wants the receiver of the message to do something that the speaker is advocating. Initial objectives might be to *introduce, modify,* or *reverse* a listener's beliefs, attitudes, opinions, or values. These objectives are all functions of the mind. The ultimate objective of the persuasive speaker is to modify behavior. Behavior modification may be an immediate, direct objective of a speaker, but, more often, the speaker is trying to alter the mindset of the listener—through influencing beliefs, attitudes, opinions, or values—in the hope that an altered mindset will bring about corresponding behavior at some future time.

If we modify an attitude, opinion, value, or belief on the topic at issue, we are creating the condition for future action. We are building up a store of potential energy in the receiver of the message that can be released at a future time, upon a given stimulus, and then becomes a kind of kinetic energy. For example, if one persuades a person to be favorably disposed to a particular political candidate, the attitude or opinion may be created one day; the potential energy (in the form of a modified or newly created attitude, opinion, belief, or value) will be stored in that person's unconscious mind, only to be released at election time. The election becomes the stimulus that triggers the action and turns the potential energy into kinetic energy. Therefore, in nearly all instances, the objective of the persuasive speaker or writer is to bring about some desired action.

The fourth basic purpose of speech, according to McBurney and Wrage (1960), is evocation. Speeches in this category are intended either to inspire or entertain. Speeches of inspiration, such as religious revival occasions, and speeches of entertainment, such as standup comedians' presentations, all contain emotional elements. Emotional elements are often a part of other types of speeches as well, but the generation of an emotion is the general purpose of a speech of evocation.

In the early twentieth century, the component parts of speech communication were subdivided into units that could be studied independently and presented in some public forum—from a high school debate contest in a classroom with four speakers and a judge to a presidential candidate's acceptance speech before millions of receivers (listeners, viewers, and readers).

Training in speech communication—especially in the United States—was usually undertaken as an extracurricular activity in high schools, colleges, and universities; however, it also became common to integrate the study of speech into the curriculum. Forensics, the formal study of speech communication, was divided into forms that emphasized style and forms that emphasized content, particularly the structure of argument. Declamation (a speech written by someone other than the speaker and delivered as a memorized public presentation) and dramatic reading (oral interpretation, originally as a memorized dramatic script) provided a focus on delivery (the use of the voice, gesture, timing, and bodily movement to maximize the emotional impact of the spoken word on an audience).

Oratory (usually written by the speaker and memorized) was characteristically presented on some ceremonial occasion and had persuasion as its primary purpose, although inspiration was often an important secondary objective. Oratory, in the Ciceronian tradition, involved accusing or defending someone in the Senate, the Assembly, or the courts, much as a prosecuting or defense attorney today would provide his summary remarks in a court of law. Because the speaker wrote his own oration, it, therefore, incorporated the elements of speech construction—determining the source of arguments and proofs, elements of composition, refutation, style, and delivery.

Debate, extempore speaking (speaking from only sketchy notes prepared during a very short preparation time), impromptu speaking (speaking off the cuff, usually with no notes, after immediately being handed a topic), and formal discussion (a group presentation in which the participants, coordinated by a leader, move the discussion of a topic through a series of sequential steps to reach a conclusion) were forensic forms that emphasized content—thesis, arguments, proofs, organization of the proofs, anticipation of counterarguments, and delivery.

This bifurcation of forensic categories into two major paths suggests the mode of thinking of those persons concerned with the characteristics of speech communication. Most speech communication analysts began to emphasize the idea, the subject matter (expressed in the thesis), arguments, and supporting evidence as a somewhat more valid area of communication study than delivery per se.

Entertainment and commemorative purposes remained significant but were suborned by the dominant purposes of information or persuasion. Keep in mind that the unified response to the symbols of the Egyptian hieroglyphs has been fractured into numerous specific areas of interest in speech communication. Studying the various facets of a subject can, of course, lead to a better understanding of the whole, but it is necessary to remember that putting the parts back together again is necessary to produce an improved, more refined whole (like a technically improved product), which we understand more fully, which allows us to be more insightful about the subject of study, and which allows us to apply its principles more effectively and honestly.

In physics, for example, numerous subdivisions of concern have solidified under the general category of classical physics, including the physical laws of Newton, Maxwell, and special and general relativity. Classical physics has bumped heads with quantum mechanics, a branch of physics that describes the activity of atomic and subatomic particles. Physicists are struggling now to reconcile the difference between classical physics and quantum mechanics. Physicists recognize that it is necessary to find a theory of everything—a fundamental theory that uniformly explains all of the physical principles of the universe.

As with classical physics and quantum mechanics, informative and persuasive messages seem to have opposing, irreconcilable differences in purpose. When one's general purpose is to inform, one creates a message that is designed to increase the receiver's pool of knowledge—facts, ideas that contain fact and opinion, images that provide new insight into a subject, facts that teach a process (the steps in doing something), set forth the historical steps in an event (chronology), place objects in space (geographic location), or to delineate the logical subdivisions of a subject (the interrelated parts of the whole). Understanding, adding ideas and facts to one's information bank, providing insight, learning the process involved in doing something (disassembling and assembling a rifle, repairing an automatic transmission of a Ford Focus)—these are the purposes of information.

Persuasion seems to be very different. A persuasive message may inform incidentally, but its primary purpose is very different from an informational purpose. A persuasive message is one that advocates a belief, position, cause, or policy. One's purpose may be to create, modify, or reverse a person's attitude, opinion, value, or belief on some topic. However, ultimately, one's objective is to motivate action in the listener or reader—to get that person to do something that will support what the sender is advocating. If we modify an attitude, opinion, value, or belief on the topic at issue, we are creating the condition for future action. We are building up a store of potential energy in the receiver of the message that can be released as kinetic energy at a future time, upon a given stimulus. For example, if one persuades a person to be favorably disposed to a particular political candidate, the attitude or opinion may be shaped well in advance of the election; the potential energy (in the form of a modified or newly created attitude, opinion, or value) will be stored in that person's mind only to be released as kinetic energy at election time. The election becomes the stimulus that triggers the action. Therefore, in nearly all instances, the objective of the persuasive speaker or writer is to bring about some desired action. It is true that even the sentence structure in a persuasive message and the sentence structure of an informative message are different. Informative messages use factual, expository statements that develop a message intended for understanding. For example, one might develop an informative thesis that states, "Three major sleep-related disorders—insomnia, narcolepsy, and apnea—all have serious negative effects on health." The speaker or writer would then develop the necessary facts, ideas, and opinions that would explain each category systematically.

Argumentative messages use sentences worded as arguments. An argument gives a reason that a particular action should be taken. For example, the proposition might say, "Voters in Fort Collins should vote for Issue 5C (to create a Larimer County library district)." Such a statement is the proposition, the action that is being called for. Each major reason used to strengthen the receiver's will and desire to take the action called for is an argument. One argument might be the following: "Forty-nine other communities have already created library districts." We know that this statement is an argument because it answers the question *Why* when applied to the idea expressed in the proposition. The proposition and argument would then read: "Voters in Fort Collins should vote for Issue 5C (to create a Larimer County library district [because] Forty-nine other communities have already created library districts." That combination of sentences makes sense grammatically and logically. That is the test of an adequate argument. The argument would then have to be supported by evidence, of course.

The example cited here is a proposition of policy, which calls for some action. The other two types of propositions—propositions of fact and propositions of value—still call for some action. A proposition of fact might state: "Resolved: That housing mortgage foreclosures will decrease next year." A proposition of value might state: "Resolved: That two years of national service for all qualified U.S. citizens is desirable." The factual statement involves the movement of a conviction from one position to another in an effort to establish the truth of a situation. The proposition of value also calls for a shift of some belief. Regardless of whether the shift is physical (the passing of a new law) or mental (the acceptance of a certain idea as desirable), action is an integral part of the process of argument. Mental movement on a concept creates a pre-condition for some future physical action. The specific action taken will depend upon the previous movement of idea.

The differences between expository and argumentative forms of expression and purpose may make it seem as if the divide between the two forms is irreconcilable, like the divide between classical physics and quantum mechanics. It is true that in teaching speech or writing, it is desirable to draw a clear distinction between these basic message structures—for the sake of clarity and simplicity. As is the case with the classical-quantum divide, it is also desirable in both spoken and written communication to look for a theory of everything. The question is whether there is a unifying element that underlies and binds the diverse components of spoken and written communication.

In fact, all elements of communication have a persuasive function; they are all concerned with change through some action. An informative speech or essay has both an agenda-setting function and a framing function. If people are exposed to lectures or informative speeches on astrophysics—whether in the college classroom or in the media—they will become increasingly aware of the points of interest of astrophysicists. Such awareness does not necessarily require extensive knowledge of the subject matter; the mere fact that people hear a subject being discussed makes them aware of this subject and moves this subject up in the hierarchy of areas of concern in the mind. This is the result of agenda-setting. Bernard Cohen (1963) provided this definition of agenda-setting theory:

> The press is significantly more than a purveyor of information and opinion. It may not be successful much of the time in telling people what to think, but it is stunningly successful in telling its readers what to think *about*. And it follows from this that the world looks different to different people, depending not only on their personal interests, but also on the map that is drawn for them by the writers, editors, and publishers of the papers they read. (13)

In addition, the particular aspects of the universe that are chosen for study suggest the relative significance of one part of the universe as opposed to another. Heavy expository emphasis on the composition, function, and effect of black holes will frame black holes as a highly important part of the universe. To the extent that the spotlight of interest shines on black holes, other significant aspects of the universe are relegated to the stage shadows—the composition, function, and effect of dark matter, for example, or the regenerative effect of quasars in a young universe.

This direction of emphasis on a subject—even a completely informative one—frames the way that the receivers of such messages see a phenomenon, such as the nature of the universe. Framing is defined by Entman (2004) as ". . . selecting and highlighting some facets of events or issues, and making connections among them so as to promote a particular interpretation, evaluation, and/or solution" (5). Both agenda-setting theory and framing theory move the minds of the receivers of informative messages in one direction or another to create their conception of physical reality. Therefore, all messages that are received by a sender (there must be a listener or a reader as well as a speaker or writer) have a persuasive function.

Persuasion, then, is the common element in all spoken and written communication. This is not to suggest that no distinction should be drawn between persuasive and informative statements of purpose and sentence wording when teaching speech communication or writing. It is to say, however, that the fact that persuasion is occurring in one form or another in all verbal and nonverbal communication should influence the analytical process of all spoken and written messages. Evaluating messages as "good" because they are informative rather than persuasive or "bad" because they—directly or indirectly—are persuasive rather than informative is a technique that results in little more than the expression of a personal opinion. The evaluation is subjective, shallow, and will often lead to invalid conclusions.

It is certainly true that dividing a subject into its component parts so that those parts can be studied and better understood as parts of the whole is valuable in the study of any discipline. It is also desirable, however, not to become preoccupied with a particular part so as to lose sight of the unifying theme of the whole. Putting the several divisions of speech communication and expository and argumentative writing together again restores the sense of "magic" and unity of symbols and their associated images that were felt by the ancient Egyptians as they contemplated their hieroglyphs.

FUNCTION OF MODERN COMMUNICATION

Today, recent traditions of the study of spoken and written communication color our view of those elements that are "good" or "bad" in current communication. In journalism, objectivity has been the defining characteristic of the discipline for more than a century. In recent years, the concept of subjectivity and interpretation made inroads into the underlying principle of objectivity.

In academe, communication has been marked by scholarly description of historical events, analysis of the results of empirical investigations, the description of processes, among others, and setting aside, for the moment, expression in the creative arts (poems, novels, short stories, and screen plays).

Business communication often involves persuasive communication. Smith (1993) notes that the marketing mix involves persuasive communication to an organization's customer base—selling, advertising, sales promotion, direct marketing, publicity, including public relations, sponsorship, exhibition, corporate identity, packaging, point of sale, merchandising, and word of mouth.

Communication theories underlying marketing include two-way communication, not only sending targeted messages to select audiences, but also conducting research on the nature of the audience response to the messages, with a subsequent refinement of the sender's message, in a continuing process of message creation and feedback. (Feedback is that information returned to the sender by the receiver that is intended, specifically, for use by the sender in evaluating the effectiveness of the sender's message.) The term *feedback* should not be confused with the generally understood meaning of the term to refer to the total return message of a receiver to a sender in a dyadic exchange of messages. The total return message is the return flow of a primary message. Feedback is a secondary flow of information that has the specific function of indicating the strengths and weaknesses of a sender's message. It is like the information about an object's position in space received by an unmanned spacecraft that allows it to correct its path on its way to a planet or some other object in space (see Wiener, 1954, 25-27 and 58-59).

Marketing communication also stresses use of non-verbal and non-symbolic ways of message creation. The picture of a certain type of person using a particular product immediately associates the product with the user. The use of space and time conveys certain impressions. In western cultures, the use of time suggests the characteristics of a person. A busy person who is also well organized provides a sense of efficiency and, thus, authority. Small, crowded areas (such as a living room or office) suggest poverty and powerlessness; on the contrary, spacious, well-organized areas suggest wealth or power.

The field of semiotics suggests ways in which symbols and signs are used in communication. *Semiosis* refers to our ability to interpret and use signs. We interpret and use signs based on our knowledge of *semiotics* (sign systems). These sign systems are developed from previous experiences in physical reality (actual physical experience in the world) and from virtual reality (images experienced on a screen). An interpretation of sign systems is a *situated activity*. It occurs in social environments that, in turn, *shape* and are *shaped by* our interpretation of signs. This is a process that occurs in the unconscious mind (*reflexive*). Advertising makes rich use of the principles of semiotics to encourage audiences to perceive images stimulated by certain symbols.

Various communication models suggest message construction opportunities for the marketer. The basic model of communication involves a sender, a message, and a receiver, with the message traveling directly from the sender to the receiver in a one-way flow of information. This model often makes some erroneous assumptions that the sender is active, that the receiver is passive, and that the message will be properly understood. Mass communication is still an attractive tool for marketers. Television offers the opportunity to display one's products in high definition, vivid color, and wide-screen realism. Radio offers a relatively low-cost opportunity to introduce or reinforce an advertiser's name, brand, and product or service line. With the internet, messages can be targeted at individuals or small, homogeneous demographic groups. Therefore, many of the principles of direct marketing can be extended to a network of electronic communication.

Four related models of communication are still used as guides for certain marketing messages. The single-step communication model (the hypodermic needle model) is seldom used these days. It says that the sender sends a message to receivers indiscriminately, with no special effort at targeting. The hypodermic needle theory assumes that the sender is capable of influencing an unthinking and non-interacting audience (see Rogers, 1983, 285-286 and Katz and Lazarsfeld, 1955).

Katz and Lazarsfeld's (1955) two-step model introduced the filter factor of the opinion leader in the equation and refined the earlier one-step communication model. The two-step model assumes that opinion leaders serve as filters in the process of influencing mass media messages. These opinion leaders interact with groups to which they belong and, thereby, influence attitudes, opinions, and values directly through interpersonal communication (see Rogers, 1983, 285-286 and Katz and Lazarsfeld, 1955).

The third communication model assumes a multi-step flow of messages from a mass communication source to receivers (see Littlejohn, 2002, 314 and Rogers, 1983, 284-286). Some of the information reaches receivers through opinion leaders; other information reaches receivers directly. In this model, opinion leaders may filter information that might have an effect on their attitudes and opinions, but one can't rely on the filter factor in all instances. A refinement of this model introduced the effect of noise in the channel that could alter the nature of the message. The same refinement introduced the concept of feedback from the receivers to the sender. The second and third models are still useful guides for marketing communication. Marketers now usually use a mix of channels to convey their messages to targeted markets.

The fourth communication model that is useful for marketers is the innovation diffusion model (Rogers, 1983). This model traces the mental process that people go through in deciding whether (and when) to adopt a product or service newly introduced into the marketplace. This model is useful for marketers because it discusses the process of *awareness, interest, evaluation, trial,* and *adoption.* Different approaches in message construction are usually used for each step in the adoption process (see Rogers, 1983, 132-134).

Marketing, journalism, broadcasting, advertising, commercial internet applications, public relations have all created schools of communication, each with its own philosophy, its own belief in the justness of its cause. This is useful for each school; it helps people concentrate on their own discipline and refine message construction and transmission to achieve their particular objectives. However, the cocoon that wraps around the practitioners of each school is often exclusionary. Each believes in the rightness of its approach to communication and, often, in the inferiority of the other schools.

PROPAGANDA AS PERSUASION

We have seen how the study of communication began with a mythical respect for the image and the symbol as a whole (the hieroglyphs of ancient Egypt) and then spread outward in an array of diverging lines, each representing the disciplinary subdivisions of communication as a whole. It is important to remember that all communication is essentially persuasive. It may persuade through an intentional application of the principles of dialectic and rhetoric, or it may persuade—at its most objective, informative level—by setting the agenda for thought and mental attention and by framing idea—through word and image—to let us see the world from one point of view instead of another. Therefore, what is the role of propaganda in society? Often-heard phrases, such as "That's nothing but propaganda" or "We must protect ourselves against propaganda" suggest that propaganda consists of blatant lies or intentional or unintentional deception. All such statements would lead us to believe in falsehoods, instead of the truth, in beliefs that subtly (and deviously) undermine our value system. And, because these messages are sneaky and invisible, we fear that they may destroy us without our knowing it. What we fear most is the unknown.

We live in a sea of persuasive messages—from the mundane to those intended to save our planet. Propaganda is part of that persuasive mix. A blanket condemnation of propaganda as evil per se closes our minds to a part of our reality and thus creates a knowledge gap. A major criticism of propaganda is that it is nothing but a pack of lies and that lies are necessary for propaganda. Of course, lies need to be exposed as such, with a corresponding revelation and chastisement of the liar. If messages are determined to be lies, the sender of the message can soon be discredited. Lies discovered in court proceedings result in a contempt charge by the judge. In the larger public sector, other "judges" need to screen messages for a contradiction of fact. This responsibility rests with the press, certain think tanks, academia, or interest groups concerned with the public welfare. A distinction needs to be drawn between a fact and intentions or interpretations. Ellul (1965) states the following:

> It seems that in propaganda we must make a radical distinction between a fact on the one hand and intentions or interpretations on the other; in brief, between the material and the moral elements. The truth that pays off is in the realm of *facts*. The necessary falsehoods, which also pay off, are in the realm of *intentions* and *interpretations*. (53)

Fact needs to be evaluated for accuracy or inaccuracy. Value and belief cannot be evaluated in the same way. Ellul (1965) says, "Propaganda is necessarily false when it speaks of values, of *truth,* of *good,* of *justice,* of *happiness*—and when it interprets and colors facts and imputes meaning to them" (59).

However, propaganda doesn't need to consist of lies, and propagandists have increasingly come to realize this. Manipulation through lies is bound to result in the defeat of the propagandist's communication objective. Moreover, a deliberate lie is likely to be exposed over time. Propaganda may use the truth to tap the (usually) unconscious reservoir of typifications and stereotypes that anchor our composite collection of beliefs and values.

The strict definition of a lie, of course, involves a false statement deliberately presented as being true. However, the question of truth or falsity in a statement is a slippery eel. If a communicator withholds some information, in what otherwise is a true statement, does that constitute a "lie"? Is the intention to deceive "a little bit" less pernicious than the intention to deceive "quite a bit"? If so, where does one draw the line?

The direct lie is more sinister than the withholding of information. If believed, the direct lie tends to throw investigators off the track. If an investigator thinks that he has the truth, he will probably stop his search and assume that the facts before him are true and reason from the untruth. If information is withheld, experts in the field may reveal gaps in the story, and investigators will want to fill in those gaps so that the picture of an event can assume an accurate and truthful whole.

The next step up the ladder involves emphasizing the positive aspects of a situation and de-emphasizing its negative aspects. This practice is nearly universal and is seldom subject to an ethical challenge. For a man, on the telephone, to try to impress a woman who doesn't know the man well, the man would very likely stress his strong points—personality, character, and, perhaps, financial stability. To emphasize the negative points would certainly result in failure to accomplish his objective. This principle applies to writers of résumés, suitors, advertisers, politicians, and to nearly everyone else. Most messages are structured to color—even if ever so slightly and even if unintentionally—the picture that the message imparts. For persuasion to be effective, a communicator will feel compelled to put his best foot forward. It really is only in this way that progress can be made, that positive action can be taken.

Persuasive language specifically intended to support a given objective is considered completely ethical and has been formed into the highly respected profession of law. Lawyers represent a client and use truthful language to promote the client's interest as fully as possible. The opposing attorney, of course, represents his client in the same confrontational manner. A judge (or jury) must determine where the weight of the evidence lies and in what way justice would best be served.

A second large organization that represents clients in much the same way that law represents its clients is public relations. Assuming no intentional effort to lie, effective and ethically defensible persuasion is nearly synonymous with effective and ethically defensible public relations. Miller (1989) says, "communication, and in this instance, persuasion, is humankind's primary symbolic resource for exerting control over the environment" (45-46).

Control of the environment has positive objectives—to make life easier, more productive, safer, and more congenial for human life and interaction. "Control," Miller (1989) notes, "[should be given] a much broader meaning . . . to say that people seek to control their environments recognizes the patently obvious fact that people . . . have a preference for certain environmental outcomes over others" (46). For example, Miller (1989) says, "From birth to death, people seek warmth rather than chilling cold; full bellies rather than empty ones; and respect, affection, and love rather than contempt, social isolation, and hatred" (46).

It is true that control doesn't depend entirely on the manipulation of symbols; nevertheless, the formation of attitudes, opinions, beliefs, and values is dependent upon the use of symbols, and symbols are the building blocks of the attitude/value/belief structure. Attitudes, opinions, values, and beliefs almost always play a central role in the life process itself, and Miller (1989) supports this idea when he says, "Whenever control of the environment hinges on the attitudes and behaviors of others, attempts to control those attitudes and behaviors are inevitable" (47).

Persuasion is also an integral part of the political process. In a democracy, politicians hold office as a result of persuasive campaigns. Even in totalitarian societies, a government will usually conduct persuasive campaigns to build support for the government, to encourage a sense of solidarity, and to shape the image of the ideal citizen of that society. In effect, public relations should be held to essentially the same standards as the law. Bald-faced lies need to be exposed; half-truths need to be revealed for what they are; polishing certain truths, while leaving others tarnished (spin), should be recognized as an inevitable part of the persuasive process and evaluated as such.

Persuasion is also an integral part of propaganda. In this case, governments (and, sometimes, other organizations) use persuasion to promote a political idea, to reinforce some societal value, to create a negative image of an enemy, or to instill fear or hatred of an enemy. Public relations, marketing, advertising, and, yes, even propaganda all use persuasive messages to encourage recipients of the persuader's message to behave in a manner consistent with the persuader's interests.

In sum, one may note the parallels in persuasive modes of communication. The legal profession represents and promotes the interests of its clients. The lawyer's job is to make the case for the client as strong as it can be. The public relations counsel is similar to that of the attorney, to represent the interests of a client (see Bernays, 1923, 50). The term "counsel" in public relations is borrowed from the legal field. Bernays (1923) describes the public relations counsel as a ". . . pleader to the public of a point of view. It is in this capacity both in interpreting the public to his client and to interpreting his client to his public [*sic*]" (Interview, PRSA, 1991). Bernays (1991) also said, "People power is the most dominant force in any society" (interview, PRSA, 1991). Bernays was thinking primarily of a democratic society. Nevertheless, the public forms a force in any society and is an entity that needs to be cultivated regardless of the political mechanism that controls societal behavior. Propaganda emphases may change somewhat from society to society, but the basic persuasive objective remains the same.

The role of the propagandist is very similar to the role of the public relations counsel. The propaganda practitioner represents a client, usually a government or an organization that represents some broad public interest, such as a union or an association [for example, the North American Free Trade Association (NAFTA)]. Bernays' definition of a public relations counsel applies equally to the propaganda practitioner: ". . . a pleader to the public of a point of view. Everything depends on the consent of the people—the engineering of consent" (interview, PRSA, 1991). In an interview with Bill Moyers, Bernays was asked whether propaganda was an evil or a legitimate function of communication science. With a twinkle in his eye, Bernays said, "The propaganda [used during WWI] was very effective, and, as I say now, it was 'proper-ganda,' not 'improper-ganda'" (TV interview, 1983).

Each communication organization in society has its own distinctive role. The journalist's role is to identify occurrences that disturb societal equilibrium. To be comfortable, people need to sense that they are in a condition of homeostasis. A homeostatic condition allows people to function in a habitual way without having to activate their thought processes. If the status is disturbed, then the fight/flight hormones are activated and the mind assumes a problem/solution state. A disturbance requires energy; the expenditure of energy requires work. The mind works if it needs to protect its host or act in some way to restore equilibrium. The journalist identifies disturbances and reports them for the edification of society. The journalist may also analyze, editorially, societal problems as well.

Academe is another large communication organization. In addition to transmitting knowledge and wisdom to receivers (students), the academy is (usually) responsible for advancing knowledge of the various curricular disciplines through objective means—verifiable research that is published in some form. Juried research is intended to assure the maximum amount of accuracy and objectivity in the ideas intended to push the envelope of knowledge.

The attorney's message construct is persuasive, as noted, and his job is to promote the interests of his client. Veracity of the information is an expectation within the ethical construct of legal communication. However, messages are tailored to promote the client's interests. This makes the communication objectives of law essentially different from the communication objectives of academe.

The public relations counsel's objective is very similar to that of the lawyer. Whereas the attorney represents a client (person, group, or organization) in a conflict based in law, the public relations counsel represents a client in a conflict or in the creation of an image that would benefit the influential interests of the client organization. The field of interest of the public relations counsel is the public sector—an organization in relation to its business or societal interest groups. Image creation is central here.

The propagandist functions much like the public relations practitioner. The organizations or interests that the propagandist represents are usually governments or societies based on similar common value systems, such as Anglo-America or the (former) Soviet Union. The objectives and techniques of the propagandist and the public relations practitioner are so similar that governments or special interest groups may employ public relations firms to promote governmental interests (as was the case with Kuwait, represented by the American public relations firm, Hill & Knowlton, in 1990, and as was the case with Belarus, which hired the British public relations firm, Bell Potting, in 2008).

Although propaganda may have specific strategic objectives, such as demoralizing enemy troops on the battlefield, its more important long-range function is to introduce, reinforce, or modify a society's values and belief structure. Reinforcement of a society's core value system is of primary concern in domestic propaganda. Introduction of core values tends to be the overriding objective in propaganda directed at foreign countries whose value systems contain elements contradictory to the values of the originating state. Modification of core value systems is usually of greater concern in foreign propaganda but may have a role in domestic propaganda as well.

PROPAGANDA'S USE OF
THE SOCIAL CONSTRUCTION OF REALITY

Our perception of reality is constructed moment by moment in our lives through the numerous messages that we receive from those who influence us. These influences come from institutions with which we are associated—the family, the school, the church, the playground, and others. We are also influenced by the messages that we receive through literature, the press, the military, the courts, and governmental bureaucracies. From these sources, we not only learn factual information and process information (the steps in doing something), but we also absorb a set of values that we usually process and store unconsciously. It is, of course, true that values can be taught directly and consciously—from our family members, our church, our school, and, sometimes, from other sources. However, even if we learn certain values directly and consciously, the condensation of the idea into the minimal number of parts that allow us to identify that idea as a part of our identification of who we are is stored as a small packet, in effect, in the unconscious recesses of the brain. Collectively, these packets become the source of our values and beliefs and allow for quick pattern recognition. Wilson (2002) notes,

> The adaptive unconscious is [a] . . . system designed to scan the environment quickly and detect patterns, especially ones that might pose a danger to the organism. It learns patterns easily but does not unlearn them very well; it is a fairly rigid, inflexible inferencemaker. It develops early and continues to guide behavior into adulthood. (66)

The process of picking up key identifying elements (the skeleton) of an idea or concept and condensing them into tiny, storable units (packets) in the brain, ready for automatic recall to the conscious mind upon a given, associated external stimulus, applies to the full realm of our value and belief system. This includes *schemas* (a pattern imposed on complex reality or experience to assist in explaining it, mediating perception, or guiding response); *typifications* (a skeletal stored impression of something that is represented by an image, a form, or a model); *stereotypes* (a stored set of unconscious fragments that provides a fixed, unvarying form to something); *profiling* (the process by which data are accumulated, placed in patterns, and then analyzed for meaning); and *framing* (the arrangement of experience into packets of information that are organized into patterns, stored in memory, and retrievable from memory at will). Wilson (2002) says,

> [An] example of automatic thinking is the tendency to categorize and stereotype other people. When we meet someone for the first time, we pigeonhole them [sic] according to their race or gender or age very quickly, without even knowing that we are doing so. This process of automatic stereotyping is probably innate; we are prewired to fit people into categories. (53)

The values and beliefs stored in the brain of a single individual are similar to those of other individuals in the same society, because collective value systems have similar characteristics. Cheung and Chan (June 2008) note, "Culture is defined by Hofstede (2001) as 'the collective programming of the mind which distinguishes the members of one human group with another'" (Quoted in Cheung and Chan, 224). Cheung and Chan (2008) continue, "Most people in the same culture carry the same values, with a value being defined as 'a broad tendency to prefer certain states of affairs over others' (Hofstede, quoted in Cheung and Chan, 18). Values are the essence of culture because these values are embedded in people's attitudes and beliefs" (224).

The message flow from propaganda is persuasive, as previously noted. Yet, the message flow of propaganda may have several purposes, sometimes selectively, sometimes in combination. Political propaganda involves techniques intentionally used by a government, a political party, or a pressure group in an effort to change the behavior of the public. Long-term effects may not necessarily be an objective. What Ellul (1965) calls sociological propaganda refers to the penetration of an ideology by means of its sociological context. Ellul (1965) says,

> Such propaganda is essentially diffuse. It is rarely conveyed by catchwords or expressed intentions. Instead it is based on a general climate, an atmosphere that influences people imperceptibly without having the appearance of propaganda; it gets to man through his customs, through his most unconscious habits. It creates new habits in him; it is a sort of persuasion from within. (64)

If propaganda is to change an environment, it must involve a continuous flow of information, offered subtly and gently. Sociological persuasion becomes the theoretical cosmological constant in the universe. As with the hypothetical physical cosmological constant, the messages of persuasion must exert a steady energy and pressure on the target societies (or the world as a whole) in which the values and beliefs of the communicator must be infused in the messages in the form of a *Weltanschauung* (a particular view of the world) and diffused through all media forms—informational programming, including news programming, and the full gamut of entertainment programming, from music videos to dramatic programming.

This infusion of propaganda need not be intentional; its intention need not be sinister; and, often, those elements of propaganda may not be recognized as such by the message creators. When an author writes a screen play, the characters that he draws, the values that they hold, the clash of values or interests that result in the story's climax, the way that the conflict is resolved all come from the author's own experience and the composite set of values that he has formulated and stored in his adaptive unconscious. Those values arise from a person's culture, and only a limited number of commonalities exist across all cultures. Therefore, in most cases, messages are going to be received, interpreted, and evaluated from very different perspectives.

Ellul (1965) cites a situation where propaganda occurred but wasn't necessarily defined as such or, in many cases, recognized as such. The instruments
of persuasion were diverse. Ellul:

> In the beginning, the United States had to unify a disparate population that came
> from all countries of Europe and had diverse traditions and tendencies. A way
> of rapid assimilation had to be found; that was the great political problem of the
> United States at the end of the nineteenth century. The solution was psychologi-
> cal standardization—that is, simply to use a way of life as the basis of unifica-
> tion and as an instrument of propaganda. (68)

For a country's population as a whole, the use of a logical argument—
especially based on the complete syllogism—is relatively ineffective at stir-
ring action to effect some desired change or to reinforce some existing belief.
Far more important is the emotion-laden idea that springs to consciousness
from the deep recesses of the unconscious mind. That concept evaluates the
incoming message and provides a rapid shield that protects the person's belief
structure, or it provides strengthening of already existing impulses.

The main distinction between the emerging persuasive message and the
responding person is a "we-they" dichotomy. If the sender's message falls
within the bounds of congruence with the receiver's belief system, the
message, in the body of the sender, is incorporated into the "we" category.
That decision reinforces the receiver's conviction of his own rightness in
his cause. He reverts to a state of homeostasis. If the sender's message falls
outside of the bounds of congruence with the receiver's belief system, the
sender is incorporated into the "they" category, and the receiver erects an
ideational-emotional defensive shield. The fight instinct arises and mental
war is waged.

The reaction to the stored value/belief packets in one's unconscious mind
involves pattern recognition. Such reaction is automatic. The receiver's response to the message creates a carapace around the delicate substance of
the value/belief underbelly. The fact that the reaction occurs almost instantaneously and automatically means that the reactive event involves virtually no
time and virtually no effort. Economy of time and effort is fundamental to the
self-preservation of the species. Without a quick response time, a civilization
could not survive.

Therefore, schemas, typifications, stereotypes, and profiling are essential
to human existence. Of course, patterns that arise from the unconscious mind
may be modified—or overridden and suppressed—by the conscious mind
when the automated message emerges from the unconscious to the conscious.
The operative term here is "may be." Most people follow the path of least
resistance and let the pre-set schemas control their behavior. That is easier

than asking whether pre-set values should be modified, and most people cherish their values. Those values incorporate the holders of the values more comfortably in their own social groups. Group membership is essential to one's sense of belonging and self-worth. Therefore, schemas, typifications, stereotypes and profiling are powerful forces that are central in controlling behavior—not that they can't be modified, but that the holder of the unconscious values and beliefs usually doesn't want to change that value/belief structure. What has worked in the past is just fine—"if it ain't broke, don't fix it." Moreover, the person responding to unconscious impulses is usually unaware that he is doing so. Therefore, if the propagandist wants to intrude into the value system of another society (often viewed as an opponent), he must do so with complete understanding of the value systems involved and work with the elements of the two systems—similarities, differences, reasons for the differences, and evidence to indicate that the persuader's beliefs/ values would be more beneficial to the targeted receivers than the receivers' current beliefs and values.

The unconscious mind can be rigid and inflexible. That is, old ideas are stored in a holding bin. This provides the foundation of the value and belief structure of the individual's consciousness. Wilson (2002) says, "to be sure, the adaptive unconscious can be rigid and inflexible, clinging to preconceptions and stereotypes even when they are disconfirmed" (65).

The conscious mind holds ultimate dominion over the adaptive unconscious from the standpoint of actual behavior in relation to impulse, but it takes will, time, and effort to assess the impulses of the unconscious, and it takes a denial of previous comforts (one's pre-set convictions) to effect a change. Wilson (2002) claims that the conscious mind is more flexible than the adaptive unconscious and, therefore, possesses ultimate control over response to messages; nevertheless, inertia is tremendously important here, and allowing the conscious mind to modify or reverse the unconscious mind involves an effort that most people are unwilling, or unable, to exert.

As Wilson (2002) noted previously, the adaptive unconscious allows a person to scan the environment quickly and detect patterns. Quick pattern recognition allows the brain to process incoming data almost instantaneously and decide what the appropriate response action should be, especially to patterns that might pose a danger to the organism.

In effect, the idea-image elements that form the packets of values and beliefs are a form of potential energy stored in the adaptive unconscious. An incoming message—containing some element that is congruent with the corresponding idea-image in the receiver's unconscious memory bank—triggers a reaction so that the stored idea becomes a kind of kinetic energy. That kinetic energy generates a response on the part of the receiver. The response takes the form of opposition, reinforcement, or opinionated evaluation of the original message that just emanated from the sender.

Because a value system is not impermeable, modifications and conversions may occur. It is much easier for dominant societies to govern and to exercise their will if the value base of the societies with which they interact is similar and the core values are essentially consistent with one another. This requires what Ellul (1956) calls "a propaganda of conformity" (74). Ellul adds,

> . . . [I]n Western Society it is no longer sufficient to obtain a transitory political act (such as a vote); one needs total adherence to a society's truths and behavioral patterns. As the more perfectly uniform the society, the stronger its power and effectiveness, each member should be only an organic and functional fragment of it, perfectly adapted and integrated. He must share the stereotypes, beliefs, and reactions of the group; he must be an active participant in its economic, ethical, esthetic, and political doings: All his activities, all his sentiments are dependent on this collectivity. And, as he is often reminded, he can fulfill himself only through this collectivity, as a member of the group. Propaganda of integration thus aims at making the individual participate in his society in every way. It is a long-term propaganda, a self-reproducing propaganda that seeks to obtain stable behavior, to adapt the individual to his everyday life, to reshape his thoughts and behavior in terms of the permanent social setting. (75)

The propaganda that Ellul (1956) is discussing here is what he refers to as broad-based sociological propaganda. This is to be distinguished from the short-term effects of psyops (psychological operations), usually employed within the military. The basic difference between sociological propaganda and psyops is that "Psyops or Psychological operations are those which 'alter the behavior of an enemy, without altering his beliefs' (those which alter beliefs are propaganda techniques)" (SourceWatch, 2008, 1). Psyops refers to narrow tactics that apply primarily to combatants and key political figures. The purpose of such propaganda is to reduce morale and cause fatal hesitation or tactical error. Despite their difference, both psyops and sociological propaganda are persuasive techniques that have behavior modification as the basic objective. Therefore, the fundamental purpose and basic argumentative structure are not different; they may be classified in the same general category.

Sociological propaganda, on the other hand, has long-range objectives and envisages long-term or permanent change. This involves working with a set of values and beliefs that may be considered something like a bed—a place of comfort, a place of rest, a place of security, a place of safety. There is a kind of luxuriousness to this bed, this resting place.

The luxurious cradle relaxes one's defenses and allows for vicarious identification with characters and events in a virtual world, characters and events with which the viewer or reader can identify. Such identification allows a person to experience (psychologically) the full gamut of emotions, ideas, and values expressed by the images and events on a screen (or in the pages of a book). Once the receiver's resistance has been lowered through a suspension of disbelief, the receiver is as open as possible for an influence on his values.

The vicarious identification is facilitated by the fact that the characters and situations in many popular screen series ease the spectator into a world of wish, desire, hope, power, and security through characters and situations that lift the self into a higher class—a class of apparent power, wealth, exercise of will, influence, security, and personal sexual attractiveness. Through vicarious identification, the viewer (or reader) loses himself in the character, becomes the character, and enjoys the surroundings of luxury in a world of virtual reality.

It is necessary to remember that the world of psychological (virtual) reality is different from the world of physical reality. Physical reality is often a world of struggle, fatigue, unrealized goals, powerlessness, subservience, personal rejection, defeat, and a constant struggle to rise again from the ashes of defeat. The ability to shed the agony of struggle and ease the sense of self into a world of virtual reality allows for a sense of self-fulfillment, self-realization, and a sense of security through the ability to control one's environment. For a moment, the reality of the self dissolves into the reality of the imagination— the reality of hope.

As one dissolves into the world of virtual reality, the sense of self is both strengthened (through a moment of psychological respite) and deceived (through escape from physical reality). Yet, the time spent in the world of virtual reality is measured by values, and the values of the virtual world may influence the set of values bound together in the adaptive unconscious of the person who dwells in the world of physical reality. That is the persuasive role of movies, television dramatic series, and the novel. For America, its cultural exports are central in its persuasive effort to spread Americanization throughout the world. The world of propaganda is subtle, but powerful. It is the task of the propagandist to identify the values of the opponent and to devise messages that will appeal to his perception in the world of virtual reality and—in the long run—to influence the receiver's value structure in his adaptive unconscious.

It must be remembered that messages are conveyed from sender to receiver not only in the form of text, but also in the form of non-verbal transference of idea, image, or emotion. That means that not just broadcast or print messages have persuasive potential, but also movies, contact with Americans through organizations such as the Fulbright Program, USAID (United States Agency for International Development,) the Peace Corps, the telephone, e-mail messages, and blogs. Person-to-person contacts convey lasting images and impressions of people and impressions that reflect a person's value system.

Elements of the value system need not always be conveyed verbally; they often may simply be inferred. However the perceptions are received, some response is likely—reinforcement of existing values (if the values of the other are contradictory to one's own), modification of one's values (if some elements of the other's value system seem to fit more congruently with some elements of one's own value system so that one's own value system can achieve a maximum state of harmony), or, rarely, a complete replacement of one's own value system (if another value system would seem to allay one's fears and fulfill one's needs and interests more effectively than the system that one currently holds).

Domestic propaganda is often produced unintentionally. We choose words that have an inherent connotation that contains the seeds of our own understanding of the world, our own perception of the world, and our own feeling about our perceptions. Whenever we use those words (whether in interpersonal communication or through electronic or textual transmissions), we are strengthening our perceptions of the idea, which reaches down to the corresponding schema, typification, and stereotype in the adaptive unconscious and strengthens it there as well.

The screen (or book) images with which one identifies vicariously not only serve as escape from the stress, strain, and boredom of physical reality, but they also serve as a model which can whet aspirations and re-ignite motivation, hope, and a sense of direction. The image and the emotion infused in that image can serve as a refined goal that can be translated into directed effort in the world of physical reality. There is a constant interplay between the world that exists in the imagination and the world that plays itself out every day as we ply the routine of physical reality. This active interaction means that new images in the imagination can provide a sense of opportunity, a sense of direction, and motivation to bring about change in the affairs of one's sensuous daily activity.

Much of the value component of these concepts tends to shift a person automatically into one camp or another. We come to feel more a part of *our* camp and distanced from *their* camp. Having membership in our camp reinforced increases our sense of security and self-importance. One says to one's self, "I have just done something to strengthen our group." A sense of self-righteousness is added to the kernel of idea/belief/emotion when one senses that one has scorned the opponent and distanced oneself from the unpleasant "other," who is often the "enemy." These constant reinforcements of ourselves in our own image make acceptance of the other group very difficult and, moreover, tend to create a dichotomous image between the self and the other that extends the distance of understanding between them and alienates one group from the other.

Several examples of value-laden words that are used freely in journalistic, academic, and interpersonal contexts have been cited in previous chapters, but one example here reveals the direction and power of value-laden word groups. In one's home country, references to one's own soldiers often refer to "our boys." "Boys" are young, strong, determined, focused, fearless warriors. This idea is condensed into its skeletal form for transference to the adaptive unconscious. The condensed kernel of the stored image is that we are safe behind that phalanx of power, and we are reassured by the feeling that we are the "best" society. Most people and societies strive to be #1.

The second thing that the phrase "our boys" does is to unify the individual and the brave boys in one's own group. There is a sense of solidarity, security, and comfort in one's own group. The group binds people of like type and like values together.

"Their" soldiers may often be described as "cold-blooded killers," "sneaky," "deceptive," "treacherous," "determined to get their ruthless way at any cost" (including suicide bombing and the saturation mining of populated land areas with anti-personnel mines and massive use of IEDs (improvised explosive devices) along roadways. We again condense these characteristics into skeletal fragments (or bundles) that we store in our unconscious minds. This, again, becomes a typification—a stereotype—that is difficult to dislodge and that immediately generates a wall of rejection and an associated emotion (usually hatred).

Unless there is a countervailing force to alter a typification, the rush of the typification to consciousness has two simultaneous effects. First, it strengthens one's own belief or value. Second, it strengthens the wall of rejection in relation to the other party. Only if some mitigating force intervenes at the conscious level will the unconscious typification or stereotype be modified. Modification is possible through logical argument, through empathizing with a relevant image, through fear of a relevant image, or through experiencing the image of a character—through vicarious identification—undergoing a series of events that cast a modifying light on the character's personality in relation to one's own. The consciously modified image of the object in question may become a new schema, typification, or stereotype that becomes recessed in the belief/values bundles in the adaptive unconscious. However, although stereotypical images can be modified, behavior change that contradicts the stereotype is usually directed by the conscious mind, which forces an override of the recessed stereotype. Behavior may be changed through an exercise of the conscious will, but a deeply rooted stereotype, formed early in life, tends to linger permanently in the recesses of the unconscious mind.

With these provisions in mind, one should be able to start organizing a grand design for a persuasive campaign, regardless of whether the persuasive objective is targeted domestically or targeted abroad. One must list, study, evaluate and understand the core values of the target audience. Likewise, one must list, study, evaluate, and understand the core values of the home society. These sets of core values must be measured, each against its opposite number in the target audience list. It is only when a home core value can be compared with its target audience counterpart and demonstrated to be more effective will a persuasive campaign be built on a solid influential foundation. Once an overall strategy is in place, the next step is to develop a specific campaign that will allow for a systematic direction of words and images to the receivers in the most effective way possible.

A propaganda effort based on core values, where long-range sociological objectives are important, necessitates a multi-pronged approach requiring a grand strategy and then specific campaigns that allow for the execution of each phase of the grand strategy. Once the task has been narrowed and focused, the propagandist must determine the program elements that will make up the campaign, the channels that will be used to transmit the message, anticipated noise that might interfere with the accurate transmission of the message, and the accessibility of receivers for the message. If possible, a mechanism should be put in place to analyze one's effectiveness at reaching the target audience and influencing the members' value/belief structures. That feedback will allow one to prepare counter-persuasive strategies and campaigns that can be used as follow-up efforts (counterattacks that can respond to the specific objections or hesitations of the target receivers).

It is easy to neglect the full range of conscious thought and unconscious impulse in preparing a persuasive strategy, and, yet, the successful propagandist should remain constantly aware of the collective unconscious. As Jung (1923) said,

> The great problems of life—sexuality, of course, among others—are always related to the primordial images of the collective unconscious. These images are really balancing or compensating factors which correspond with the problems life presents in actuality. This is not to be marveled at, since these images are deposits representing the accumulated experience of thousands of years of struggle for adaptation and existence. (271)

One must not underestimate the difference in levels of resistance and obscurity of the conscious and unconscious minds. Those values stored in the unconscious mind are stubborn; they are resistant to change; and they are often not clearly understood through analysis in the conscious mind. This makes the knee-jerk reaction that arises from an incoming propaganda message difficult to control and often difficult to understand. Jung (1968) says, "The conscious mind allows itself to be trained like a parrot, but the unconscious does not—which is why St. Augustine thanked God for not making him responsible for his dreams" (51).

The perception that the bundles of condensed value and belief that form our schemas, typifications, and stereotypes suggests that there is something sinister and ultimately destructive in the unconscious fragmented patterns that can spring into consciousness upon an appropriate stimulus.

Jung (1966) supports the idea that the schemas, typifications, and stereotypes are not inherently evil or always result in negative behavior. In reality, the skeletal packets of belief/value systems, stored in the unconscious, are neutral entities in and of themselves. Their manifestation in the conscious mind contains the potential to have positive results as well as negative results. Jung (1966) says,

> The unconscious is not just evil by nature, it is also the source of the highest good: not only dark but also light, not only bestial, semihuman, and demonic but superhuman, spiritual, and, in the classical sense of the word, "divine." (364)

Movement of people from one camp to another may not necessarily have negative consequences. Strengthening one's sense of belonging to one's own group may be positive; however, when conflict exists between one's own group and the other, the typification and the stereotype are likely to produce counterproductive results.

REFERENCES

Aristotle. The rhetoric of Aristotle. Trans. J.E.C. Weldon, 1886. London: Macmillan. Elibron Classics reprint. Adamant Media 2005. www.elibron.com.

Bernays, Edward L. 1929. *Crystallizing public opinion.* New York: Horace Liveright.

———. 1983. The image makers. [Television series episode]. In Bill Moyers, *A walk through the 20th century.* WNET, New York & KQED, San Francisco: Public Broadcasting Service.

———. 1991. Video interview with Shirley A. Serini (Public Relations Society of America), August 7. Cambridge Cable: Cambridge, MA.

Cheung, Hoi Yan, and Alex W. H. Chan. 2008. Corruption across countries: Impacts from education and cultural dimensions. *The Social Science Journal,* 45(2), 223-239.

Cohen, Bernard Cecil. 1963. *The press and foreign policy.* Princeton, NJ: Princeton University Press.

Čzerný, Jaroslav. 1951. *Ancient Egyptian religion.* London: Hutchinson House. Accessed September 1, 2008, http://www.hermesthoth.org/library/Egyptian/Ancient % 20 Egyptian % 20 Religion. Pdf.

Ellul, Jacques. 1965. *Propaganda: The formation of men's attitudes.* Trans. Konrad Kellen and Jean Lerner, 1973. New York: Vintage Books.

Entman, Robert M. 2004. *Projections of power: Framing news, public opinion, and U.S. foreign policy.* Chicago: University of Chicago Press.

Hofstede, Geert. 2001. *Culture's consequences: Comparing values, behaviors, institutions, and organizations across nations* (2nd ed.). Beverly Hills, CA: Sage.

Jensen, Klaus Bruhn. 1995. *The social semiotics of mass communication.* Thousand Oaks, CA: Sage.

Jung, Carl Gustav, and Helpon Godwin Baynes. 1923. Psychological types. In *The collected works of C.G. Jung, 6.* London: Kegan Paul Trench Trubner.

Jung, Carl Gustav. 1966. The practice of psychotherapy: Essays on the psychology of the transference and other subjects. In *The collected works of C.G. Jung, 16.* Princeton, NJ: Princeton University Press.

———. 1968. Psychology and alchemy. In *The collected works of C.G. Jung* (2nd ed.): *12.* London: Routledge.

Katz, Elihu, and Paul F. Lazarsfeld. 1955. *Personal influence: The part played by people in the flow of communications.* New York: Free Press.

Littlejohn, Stephen W. 2002. *Theories of human communication* (7th ed.). Stamford, CT: Wadsworth.

McBurney, James H, and Ernest J. Wrage. 1960. *Guide to good speech* (2nd ed.). Englewood Cliffs, NJ: Prentice-Hall.

Miller, Gerald R. 1989. Persuasion and public relations: Two "Ps" in a pod. In Carl. H. Botan and Vincent Hazelton, Jr., eds, *Public relations theory*, 45-66. Hillsdale, NJ: Lawrence Erlbaum.

Psyops. (from SourceWatch). 2008, March 17. Accessed September 1, 2008, from http://www.sourcewatch.org/index.php? Title=Psychological _warfare.

Rogers, Everett M. 1983. *Diffusion of innovations* (4th ed.). New York: Free Press.

Smith, Paul R. 1993. *Marketing communications: An integrated approach.* London: Kogan.

Wiener, Norbert. (1954). *The human use of human beings.* Garden City, NY: Doubleday Anchor.

Wilson, Thomas D. 2002. *Strangers to ourselves: Discovering the adaptive unconscious.* Cambridge, MA: The Belknap Press of Harvard University Press.

Chapter Six

Propaganda:
From Theory to Practice

As important as propaganda is in shaping the values/belief structure—and, ultimately, behavior patterns—of a society, propaganda is just one mechanism, among several, that is necessary to accomplish a nation's, or society's, total persuasive objectives in relation to itself and to outside target audiences. Humanitarian efforts and, sometimes, military efforts are also part of the persuasive mix. Nevertheless, the world of idea, image, and emotion that is part of the communication process assumes an important role in defining and giving structure to values and beliefs, the bedrock of human behavior.

Again, it is good to remember that propaganda is a neutral persuasive device. It can be used whenever a country wants to strengthen and unify its own population or generate fear and hatred of an enemy. Taylor (1998) says,

> Value judgments about propaganda being a "good" or a "bad" thing . . . would more profitably be directed at the cause being advocated or the regime conducting it rather than at the process itself. In so far as the process is concerned, we can legitimately refer only to "effective" or "ineffective" propaganda. And because censorship is the Siamese twin of propaganda by virtue of the fact that it involves the exclusion of certain facts and alternative viewpoints which may prejudice the credibility of the case being made, we can see that one of the most effective forms of propaganda is that which either remains hidden or which appears in the disguise of "news" and "information." (24-25)

Propaganda is often thought of as a wartime activity, and warring nations nearly always use propaganda; indeed much can be learned about civilian uses of propaganda from sharply focused propaganda efforts during wartime. Propaganda isn't just a military tool. It is a tool that any society would want to use to provide organizational cohesiveness to achieve a maximally unified image of a nation in the minds of the populace. Without such an image, political control is very difficult. An example of the effective use of propaganda in nation building is that used by Mao Tse-tung in shaping China's post-World War II society.

However, to get some sense of the propaganda strategies used in wartime, Nazi Germany and the United States in the Gulf War will serve as examples. Actually, very sophisticated principles of propaganda go back about a century and have been used by the major players in the quarrels of the twentieth century.

The concept of the mass man was prevalent in the mid-twentieth century. It was believed that the mass man had many characteristics in common and could be persuaded uniformly by propagandistic messages. The Spanish philosopher and writer, José Ortega y Gasset (1930) expressed the thought of the time regarding the nature of the mass man. Ortega wrote,

> Strictly speaking, the mass, as a psychological fact, can be defined without waiting for individuals to appear in mass formation. In the presence of one individual we can decide whether he is "mass" or not. The mass is all that sets no value on itself—good or ill—based on specific grounds, but feels itself "just like everybody," and nevertheless is not concerned about it; is, in fact, quite happy to feel itself as one with everybody else. (14-15)

PROPAGANDA USE UNDER NATIONAL SOCIALISM

The Nazis were well aware that powerful symbols would be necessary to encourage vicarious identification with the leaders and the spirit of National Socialism. Words alone could not express the strength and success of the Nazi cause. Music, rhythm, and color give life and power to symbols and provide a deeper emotional impact than a reasoned argument alone.

The Nazis placed considerable emphasis on mass meetings, a practice that was referred to as "active propaganda." A sense of the group, and wanting to be accepted by the group, is stirred by close contact with others and responding to inspirational music of the movement, the drums, the colorful flags, and other symbols.

National unity could be encouraged by evoking some of the ceremonial practices of the people's Teutonic ancestry—flaming torches and bonfires at a nighttime lakefront. Inspiring speeches gave idea to the aroused emotion and fused idea with feeling. Nazi propaganda was founded on several basic principles. The Nazis believed that immediate sensory experience, obtained through group activity, exerts more influence on one's attitudes and beliefs than arguments do. Verbal propaganda should create the illusion of immediacy and concreteness (see Kris and Speier, 1944). The spoken word is more powerful than the written word; eyewitness accounts had more dramatic and influential impact than summary accounts of events.

Personalized news stories had more impact than academic discussions, because it is easier for listeners, viewers, and readers to identify vicariously with a dramatized presentation than with an expository presentation. "Understanding" is to be shaped by feeling. That is the reason that sensory experience constructed in story form has the greatest potential for melding idea and feeling.

The Nazis also believed that an individual was open to suggestion and that group dynamics were an integral part of group-influenced attitude formation. Repetition was an essential part of Nazi propaganda, as well as the use of charmed words, words rife with emotion but which, in themselves, stifled logical thought because the emotion drowns out the thought. Some patriotic words fall in that category, as well as some religious words.

Even though the mass couldn't generate new, progressive ideas, it, nonetheless, held great power collectively and, therefore, had to have its value and belief structure shaped in accordance with core values of the political power in control. The Nazis referred to the masses in their writings and believed that the crowd was dehumanized and inflammable. With that being the case, symbols should spark emotion—fear, love, hate, and devotion to one's country and leader. Repetition of simple, emotion-charged words and images would renew the belief, flagging over time, to new heights of power, will, and determination. Of course, one of the core values of Germany at the time was that instinct, emotion, and will were the most powerful force that would lead to a refined society and a more advanced evolutionary man. This value stood in contrast to the Anglo-American belief in reason, through the application of logic and evidence, as the main motivator of an evolving society. The Nazis seldom used the word "reason" in their propaganda. With such a value, the power of the leader is paramount, and a suggestion from the leader becomes the beacon to guide the ship of state.

The Germans were well aware of the concept of the stereotype, which had been introduced by Walter Lippmann (1922). It was the concept of a stereotype that Lippmann was describing when he referred to "a standardized picture in the head." Lippmann, however, did not distinguish between the stereotype as a stimulus and the stereotype as a response. This distinction was drawn by Allen E. Edwards (1940), who suggested that there was an interplay of the stereotype between the conscious and unconscious minds. Edwards' (1940) defined a "stereotype" as ". . . a stimulus which arouses standardized preconceptions which are influential in determining one's responses to the stimulus" (357-358). Applying Edwards' definition to German propaganda, Kris and Speier (1944) noted, "The standardized preconceptions were purposefully created by German propagandists and the stereotype is made to condense various elements of the contexts of propaganda" (33).

For example, the word "war," which is loaded with frightful elements, as well as, perhaps, determination to overcome a feared enemy, was used very little in German propaganda. The word "war" was replaced by more euphemistic phrases, such as ". . . reprisals for Polish attacks and provocations" (Kris and Speier, 33). And, of course, with an eye on euphemistic terms, the American military activities in Korea from 1950 until 1953 were never officially referred to as a "war"; they were a "police action."

The Germans were aware that a stereotype is not primarily a verbalized re-creation of an idea. It is, rather, the resurgence of an emotionally charged bundle of attack and defend stimuli. This is the protective wall around a person's cherished inner self (his values and beliefs) that has been discussed in previous chapters.

In the German analysis of propaganda technique, the stereotype doesn't refer primarily to an argument, rather to an image often created in caricature that is charged with negative emotion. (Hate is frequently conjured up in the propagandist's image, but, in some instances, it might also be love.) Kris and Speier (1944) suggest one way that the stereotype was used in Nazi propaganda:

> When the German propagandist speaks of the Jew, that word is a stereotype which evokes an image. "The picture in the head" [referring to Lippmann's use of the term in *Public Opinion* (1922)] is of something dirty, with a long nose, sensual, scheming and plotting to destroy Germany; each of its attributes is fully determined and rich in connotation, while some are interchangeable. When the Jew is poor and in rags, his revenge is dangerous; when he is rich and lives in London or Washington, his power is fearful. But it is always the same image, one of great visual vividness and high emotional charge. (35-36)

The German idea of visual and textual simplicity in a propaganda statement involves getting at the kernel of an idea, reducing it to its essential elements, painting as vivid a picture of it as possible, and keeping the meaning as simple as possible. Kris and Speier (1944) say, "In the ideal instance no inconsistent traits appear in them. The words that are to build up the image are vivid, composed like a poster, seductive, easy to remember, and meant to be 'taken for real,' but deprived of the complexities of reality . . . individual items are made to fit like stones in a mosaic" (36).

Vividness, simplicity, color, omission of detail, as in a mosaic—these qualities allow the image to assume a firm place in the unconscious mind. Reference to a mosaic calls to mind the principle of the enthymeme, discussed in chapter 2. One of the strengths of the enthymeme is that it requires the receiver of the message to fill in mentally an unstated premise. Involving an audience with a combined idea/image/emotion draws that impression into the mind of the receiver. The missing premise requires that the receiver (the audience) commit himself to finishing the impression. Requiring participation by the receiver in completing the idea/image/emotion involves the listener in the idea. He has become a partial creator of the idea, and we develop a personal attachment to that which we create.

The mosaic, too, involves a mental filling in of the blank areas around each picture element. The picture elements and the blank interstices are seen separately when one is close to the mosaic. As one moves away from the mosaic, the mind wants to eliminate the blanks and create a whole picture. At a given point, the blank interstices disappear, and the eye and brain see a whole picture; the blank spaces have disappeared.

The mental fill-in principle was very much a part of German propaganda. Kris and Speier (1944) note:

> The propagandist is convinced that his imagery has grown deep roots among the German people. He assumes that it has become so familiar that whenever he exposes only part of an image the public will supply the rest. He hopes that this tendency will be an obstacle to reasonable examination of the meaning of his words and that the urge toward completing a familiar pattern will take the place of thinking. (36-37)

For example, if a German propagandist reports on a well-known member of the opposition, whose image has already been caricatured, the mere mention of the name will generate the caricature immediately from the receiver's unconscious mind. Just prior to the outbreak of World War II, German propaganda had painted an image of Churchill as fat, old, doddering, and evil-looking. He was smoking a cigar and had a glass of whiskey in his hand. Here was a drunken criminal who enjoyed war (see Kris and Speier, 1944).

A caricature is a portrait that exaggerates or distorts characteristic features ". . . of a person or thing to create an easily identified visual likeness" (VisualWikipedia, 1). Although caricatures are usually intended to ridicule the subject, they may be complimentary. The term "caricature" is derived from the Italian *caricare*—to charge or load. Therefore, the word *caricature* essentially means a *loaded* portrait (see VisualWikipedia, 1).

The caricature is often used in propaganda. The Soviet Union used caricature frequently, both during World War II and during the Cold War that followed. The caricature exaggerates characteristic features—such as large ears, a facial scowl or bushy eyebrows—and drives home the appearance and associated emotion of the person being caricatured through building a simplified skeletal outline of a person. That skeletal outline can more easily be stored in the adaptive unconscious. The exaggerated features serve something like the picture elements in a mosaic. The exaggerated features snap together when called forth as a whole and create the distorted image with its associated emotion. Thus, the portrait is a relatively easy way of creating an emotion-charged image that resides in the unconscious and can be called to consciousness easily by an appropriate stimulus, such as the person's name.

Because conditions change over time, and because enemies and friends may exchange places, the propagandist may need to modify the image that was first created to maintain the believability of the propaganda in light of new information that becomes available to the audience. This is particularly true in wartime when the progress of the war is changing. This occured in Germany during World War II, and, as noted by Kris and Speier (1944), "The old image of the war was reedited; gradually corpses appeared in the newsreels, horror was admitted; and out of horror grew the stylized heroism at Stalingrad. The changing features of the war were absorbed into a revised image" (38).

German radio, during World War II, was divided into main broadcasting divisions: (1) news and propaganda, and (2) programming. Nevertheless, the concept of the universality of persuasion underlay all of German broadcasting. Even programming devoted to entertainment had political overtones. As Kris and Speier (1944) note, ". . . Nazi propagandists proclaimed that entertainment as such does not exist. The German radio, it was said, 'has purely political functions . . . even its cultural, entertainment, and current history broadcasts serve a higher political order'" (quoted in Kris and Speier, 1944, from Kriegler, 7-12). The Nazis sensed the universality of persuasion in communication very early.

The importance of core values in relation to a society's image of itself is essential for the propagandist to understand, cultivate, and reinforce in the creation of persuasive messages. Several of the core differences between National Socialism and the Anglo-American West were noted in chapter 4.

One core value that the National Socialists worked hard to create and then strengthen was the value of the collective self. Overcoming the value of individualism per se or of regional, rather than national, identity was a major goal of the propagandist. First, German regional identity and loyalty had to be subsumed by a national identity. Second, stress was placed on the collective self. The individual should consider himself, first and foremost, a member of the German people, or simply Germany, rather than as independent personalities—Herr Schmidt or Frau Braun. This value ran counter to the value of individualism, a core value of the Anglo-American West.

Under collectivism, the image of the individual is meant to be submerged to a collective sense of self—to being a German and being proud of one's national identity. The objective of persuasive communication, in this regard, is to encourage the individual to merge with the collective self. The collective self should weld the nation into a powerful, unified entity. The idea here is that the German is more than just a citizen of his country; he is born into the German race and tied to the actions of his country. So, what are some of the measures taken by the propagandist to promote a collective identity?

National community (*Volksgemeinschaft*) is encouraged. This entails a sense of closeness and personal trust of the members of the society. It represents a feeling of togetherness, an arms-around-the-shoulder attitude toward one's fellow countrymen as one moves uniformly together to accomplish the objectives of the nation. It has the sense of being a member of the same family. The relationship is one of mutual respect, one of feeling bound together by the same traditions, one of friendship, or one of some other cohesive social factor. The German sociologist Ferdinand Tönnies described *Gemeinschaft* as a "reciprocal, binding sentiment . . . which keeps human beings together as members of a totality" (47) (see also Tönnies, F. *Community and Society*).

The principle of *Gemeinschaft*—encouraged under collectivism—stands in sharp contrast to the principle of *Gesellschaft*, which was the "glue" binding diverse, heterogeneous populations that characterized the Anglo-American industrial West. Under *Gesellschaft,* the essential condition of the social relationship is the formal contract. The contract is binding, with legal force behind it, but not requiring any special relationship between the individuals holding the contract. According to Tönnies, the contract creates a tension between the parties holding the contract. The *Gesellschaft* creates a society for the individual in which the relationship among individuals is impersonal and anonymous. DeFleur and Ball-Rokeach (1989) say, "The *Gesellschaft* is a system of competitive relationships where individuals seek to maximize what they get from exchanges and minimize what they give, at the same time learning to be wary of others" (155).

The contrast between the principle of collectivism, propounded by the National Socialists, and the principle of Western individualism is dramatic. Yet, development and reinforcement of either core value depends upon propaganda, and the propaganda requires the use of all instruments of persuasion, not just the mass media, including the internet, but in pictures, films, music CDs, speeches, books, sermons, and even billboard advertisements. Propaganda involves a total commitment to use all of the available means of communication to build, maintain, and solidify a core value.

The propagandist must explain the necessities of life as necessities for the survival of the biological unit. As the society moves toward victory, the propagandist's reference is to the nation, not the individual. The common man living in that society feels at one with the collective movement. All of a person's contacts—his superiors at work, his family, and his friends—are marching at his side to achieve the goals of the society. As Kris and Speier (1944) note,

> To make Herr Schmidt imagine himself on the march all of the time by a process of propagandistic suggestion would be difficult indeed, were it not that whether he likes it or not his whole life is actually framed within the militarized organization of National Socialism. (167)

The German core value based on money in society also stands in sharp contrast to the values of the Anglo-American West. Under socialism, German shareholders split their profit with the community. The Anglo-American core value, based on individualism, contains the belief that whatever profits are made are in the hands of the shareholder. The only obligation to the community is through governmental taxation. German companies, under National Socialism, provided dividends of more than six percent to the community. The worker was honored, because work itself was dignified, and the product of one's hand or mind made the state what it was, and each brick in the building that is the state is a product of a worker's knowledge and skill.

Self-denial is part of the socialist core value, but so is *joy,* from which the common man gains strength. The concept of joy differs from the concept of *happiness* as expressed in the American Declaration of Independence: "We hold these truths to be self-evident, that all men are created equal, that they are endowed by their Creator with certain unalienable Rights, that among these are Life, Liberty and the pursuit of Happiness." The ability to pursue happiness is the foundation of liberty, and happiness, essentially, refers to freedom to pursue one's life objectives free from enforced constraints, the opportunity to achieve maximum health, maximum knowledge, maximum understanding, and maximum ability to move about without constraint, and to pursue the objects of one's desires. More could be said about the concept of happiness in the Declaration of Independence, but, suffice it to say, the concept of happiness as a core American value differs substantially from the National Socialist concept of *joy.* Joy is related to the internal satisfaction that comes from a personal sense of accomplishment as a participating molder of the state.

In National Socialism, the image of the enemy varied in accordance with long-standing attitudes about ethnic groups. The image painted by the propagandist was most effective when it was based on one of those stereotypical impulses. German war propaganda differentiated between two basic types of enemies. The first group consisted of persons for whom the Germans already had a long-standing contempt—the Jews, the Russians, the Poles, and the Serbs. German propaganda, at this time, depicted these groups as subhuman.

The propaganda could be relatively unidimensional, drawing on very specific and clearly formed stereotypes.

A different technique needed to be employed for nations that were part of Western civilization. Stereotypical images were less clearly formed about these groups. For example, many Germans had emigrated to America, Canada, and other countries in the Western Hemisphere. Nevertheless, the Anglo-American countries were an enemy, and, therefore, a negative image had to be created about each major player in the preparation for war. England was mentioned most frequently in German propaganda. England was the main enemy, and, according to Kris and Speier (1944), England received the most propaganda treatment because it was the "most feared" of Germany's enemies (215).

If ethnic hatred were not a stereotype, then other weaknesses and unpleasant associations would need to be found. In the case of German propaganda against England, the image of the Englishman, in radio news broadcasts, was one of weakness and many kinds of immorality. The weakness theme was intensified after the occupation of France (May 10, 1940) and at the beginning of the push to the East (Operation Barbarossa, June 22, 1941). In the early stages of the Second World War, England stood largely alone in its effort to turn back the Nazi attack on that country. A theme that ran through much of German propaganda of the time was that the English were cruel, cowards, and were bound to lose the war. The concentration on England, in German propaganda, rather than the Red Menace to the east, was probably due to the fact that the stereotypes about Bolsheviks were already deeply set in the unconscious mind and could be triggered by a few words or an image or two. Concepts such as weakness, cruelty, cowardice and a fatal sense of a self-fulfilling destiny regarding the outcome of the war are much more complex concepts than an emotionally based ethnic hatred. Such concepts have to be built first before they can become the condensed mosaic that will be stored in the adaptive unconscious as a well-formulated, emotionally charged stereotype.

France never received the amount of German propaganda that England did. A clear stereotype existed among nationalistic Germans about France, which had been Germany's historical enemy. The propaganda against England was selective in nature. There was an attack against British plutocrats, but the propaganda noted that many British people were not plutocrats. The charge of hypocrisy was also leveled against the British selectively. The brunt of that charge focused on British statesmen and spokesmen. The British common man was largely spared from such charges.

Selective propaganda is more difficult to turn into an emotionally charged element that can assume its place as a volatile stereotype than is propaganda that targets an entire population. That was the case with Nazi propaganda against the Russians. The verbal attack against the Russians contained a similar sentiment to that of some southern whites about the Negroes in those times. The Russians were considered absolute enemies, as were the Negroes, and absolute enemies are considered bestial and subhuman. Their enemies described Negroes as having the attributes of large animals: brute strength, savage lust, and no knowledge of the moral law. In Nazi propaganda, the Russians became wild beasts and formless demons. Hitler referred to them as "swamp-men" (Kris and Speier, 1944, 219-223).

Whereas an image of the enemy needs to be created and imbued with an emotional charge, so does an image of one's own personnel. The German soldier was painted in a heroic light. He was swift, efficient, vital, and considerate of others, including the enemy. As they marched into the Soviet Union, German propaganda stressed how civilized Germans were. In the event of defeat, the propagandist usually attributed it to overwhelming numbers of the enemy.

Regarding the French, German propaganda said that, although brave, the French soldiers were inconsistent in quality, and some lost their nerve. As to the Americans, German propaganda was generated only after American troops engaged German army units. The initial anti-American propaganda referred to American army units in the First World War. Hitler compared American troops unfavorably with the French and British. Rauschning (1940) notes, "They [the American troops] ran straight into the line of fire, like young rabbits," referring to American behavior in World War I (71). The American soldier was also characterized as a "wise guy," unaware of duty and "soldierly virtue" (Kris and Speier, 1944, 239).

When creating an image for propaganda purposes, the more sharply that image can be drawn and simplified, the easier it is to bring the image to the fore of consciousness. This holds true for a heroic image created of one's own leaders or of a villainous image created of an enemy leader. With some core values built into each image, the stage is set for creating a drama involving a personal conflict between two people. The pitched battle between two people is elemental and is the simplest image that depicts a conflict. A boxing match represents this idea. Two men, using fists, seek to best each other through strength and boxing skill. This is elemental drama. The scope of the activity is minimal, confined by a ring; the actions of the fighters follow a consistent pattern, round after round.

The pitting of two opposing forces against one another is probably the simplest way to create drama—and, through the generation of drama—to capture and hold attention and interest. Journalists frequently use the principle of bilateral conflict to keep the story idea clear and to generate interest in the story's context. Politicians use this principle in the horse race during a political campaign. The candidates emerging in the run for office are pitted against each other, much as are two boxers.

Propaganda benefits from this principle and is frequently used in propaganda campaigns. Personalizing the propaganda is a principle that goes back at least to Aristotle's *Rhetoric*. The principle of simplification of a contest between divergent core values is employed when the leader of a country is pitted against the leader of the opposing country (or two opposing organizations). In effect, the leader of a country is substituted for the nation as a whole.

Hitler used this device frequently. During the Czechoslovak crisis in 1938, Hitler focused his attack not on the Czechoslovak nation, but on its leader, Eduard Beneš. The personalized attack tends to be used discriminately. It is modified according to political intention. It tends to be used against enemies that are, more or less, respected. Enemies that are considered subhuman are less in need of a personalized attack. During World War II, the personalized attack focused primarily on the British and American leaders, rather than the people of Britain or the United States. Churchill and Roosevelt were cast as the foe of Germany, and the prime minister and president were made symbols of Anglo-American values and political intentions against Germany. Incidentally, no substitution took place where Russia was involved. It wasn't considered necessary when an entire category of people is considered subhuman.

Prime Minister Churchill was portrayed as a grinning fat man with a cigar protruding from his jowls. He is depicted as a cruel, lying, alcoholic warmonger. He associates with plutocrats and has aligned himself with Bolsheviks. Churchill was symbolized as the leader of a weak and disunited England.

President Roosevelt superseded Prime Minister Churchill in the German propaganda effort after America became actively involved in the war. German propaganda tried to establish a Jewish heritage for Roosevelt, but the propaganda focused primarily on Roosevelt's Jewish brain trust, the Jewish press of America, the Jewish-run broadcasting system, and Jewish party organizations. German propaganda characterized Roosevelt as a madman.

PROPAGANDA USED BY THE UNITED STATES AND IRAQ IN THE GULF WAR

In Mesopotamia, between the Tigris and the Euphrates rivers, some 4,000 years ago, the Assyrians built monuments depicting their military might. These stone monuments were placed strategically around the region and showed the ferocity of the Assyrian kings. These monuments conveyed a persuasive message intended for both domestic and foreign audiences. The theme of the message was fear—fear that would assure the docility of the population within the region and fear that would deter attack from neighboring tribes (see Taylor, 1998).

When Saddam Husein seized power in Iraq in 1979, he used propaganda that was based heavily on ancient imagery and symbolism. Saddam also used statues depicting in various poses the strength and authority of the Iraqi leader. Once again, it is important to note that the words chosen to express an idea (or even a "fact") are important elements of propaganda. In the Gulf War (1991), reports from inside Iraq to the West were flagged as being "subject to Iraqi military censorship" (Taylor, 1998, 25). When Western journalists issued reports from embedded reporters with Allied troops, it was common to note that some operational facts might be missing, but the terminology to express this idea was often words to the effect that "in this, and other reports from the Gulf, some operational facts are omitted for reasons of military security." The dichotomous we-they opposition is suggested—"they" conduct censorship, whereas "we" issue reports subject to the guidelines of operational security.

Words as propaganda are often not considered in discussions about the subject, but words, often used unintentionally, can have a strong persuasive influence. This was true of persuasive language use during the Gulf War. An air strike might be described as "effective," but, as Taylor (1998) notes, the word "effective" might not necessarily mean that a target had been destroyed. Taylor also mentions euphemistic phrases, such as "collateral damage" and "interdiction" to gloss over words that would describe the carnage of reality. Pilots returning from a flight might be described as "knights of heroic warfare," who used "smart" weapons (43). Phrases such as these color the verbal picture in the hue of the propagandist—usually unintentionally.

We use language that reflects our culture, and certain words and phrases are built into our linguistic culture. More often than not, we use these phrases unaware of the propagandist's overtone inherent in the utterance itself. The media watch-dog Fairness and Accuracy in Reporting cited several phrases used by American television journalists when reporting on the war. These phrases included the following: "from the 'brilliance' of American laser-guided bombs to the Scud as 'a horrifying weapon'" (ABC's Peter Jennings, cited in Taylor, 1998, 45). Another report said that the initial bombing of Iraq was a "marvel" (CBS's Charles Osgood, cited in Taylor, 1998, 45). The "marvel" occurred after "two days of picture perfect results" (CBS's Jim Stewart, cited in Taylor, 1998, 45).

It is almost impossible to avoid using words that color a picture of an event, both domestically and in the enemy countries. These words are part of our vocabulary, and words of substance (nouns, verbs, adjectives) carry an inherent connotation that members of a particular culture don't think of as a superimposed idea/image/emotion, because we sense that when we use a particular word, we know that it means what it says. We seldom think that the connotation of a particular word draws on the schemas in our memory banks and functions to reinforce the values of our own culture and, often simultaneously, attacks the values of another culture. It seems that, as long as there are core values in one culture that differ substantially from the core values of an opposing culture, there is little hope for sympathetic communication. If, however, a country's situation changes, some core values may change to accommodate the new conditions. For example, if a developing country has a massive impoverished class and a small wealthy elite class, core values will very likely change if that country can establish a substantial middle class where the economic viability of the members of that class will depend upon capitalistic business practices or socialistic employment opportunities, such as holding a position in government. Then, values often become adjusted to meet the new economic requirements of a consumer class. Therefore, communication per se isn't the only activity that can be built into a grand persuasive campaign. Nevertheless, communicating values is an essential part of that comprehensive persuasive effort. The use of language to develop and reinforce beliefs and values is evident in opponents' domestic propaganda. Words are not usually chosen with a propaganda effort in mind, but with the connotation of one's value and belief system emerging from the emotion of the moment. For example, in Saddam Hussein's first wartime speech to the nation, he said that the "Mother of All Battles between triumphant good and doomed evil" had begun [reported in Britain's *Daily Telegraph* (1/07/91) and quoted in Taylor, 97]. Saddam's son, Udai, reportedly sent a message to his father that said, "We sacrifice ourselves to you, symbol of Iraq and its leader . . . I am on my way to southern Iraq to join the brave lions and men of Iraq who will sacrifice themselves in defence [*sic*] of their beloved country [reported in Britain's *Guardian* (1/18/91) and quoted in Taylor, 97].

The similarity of the connotations of the words used by the "enemy" and the connotations of similar words used in "our" statements is striking. The words arise from the stored values and beliefs in the adaptive unconscious and spring forth from the value/image/emotion content of the stored, encapsulated values inherent in the particular culture involved. Although the values differ from culture to culture, the impulse to use words that have a reinforcing effect domestically and an adversarial effect in the opposing nation or culture are of the same type.

On the other side of the spectrum was the use of words with a similar type of effect by the Americans. General Walter Boomer, U.S. Marine Corps

Commander, reportedly described Saddam as a "moral pygmy" [reported in Britain's *Times* (1/28/91) and quoted in Taylor, 80]. Saudi officials called Saddam the "lord of death" and the "father of destruction" and as a "monster who had violated international, as well as Islamic law which stressed respect for the environment" [reported in Britain's *The Independent* (1/28/91) and quoted in Taylor, 80]. Each verbal attack came not only as a result of political opposition, but also as a result of differing core values. The Iraqi statements arose from the belief that the Sunnis should maintain control of a united Iraq; the American statements arose from the capitalistic value that free trade should be facilitated by open channels of commerce where the economic interests of the country are at stake.

An occasional reporter—British or American—noticed the difficulty of obtaining a legitimate picture of an event when propaganda occurs almost spontaneously in much of a society. Obtaining a comprehensive, accurate picture of an event is made much more difficult when the intentionally de-signed propaganda is intermingled with the primarily unintentional use of words and phrases with connotations that arise from the memory banks of stored schemas (or stereotypes). However, that is the world that we live in, and communication science must develop ways of filtering the information so that ideas of like type that lead to an accurate understanding of an event can be associated properly for a comprehensive understanding of that event.

What was the core value difference in the Gulf War? Iraqi propaganda described a struggle between *technology* and *faith*. Faith was strengthened by developing a historical sense of the movement of Arabs and the Islamic people. Faith was the Islamists' weapon. Iraqi propaganda indicated that faith was pitted against the Western core value of "the computer and electron-ics" [reported in Britain's *The Times* (1/23/91) and cited in Taylor, 84-85]. Saddam Hussein, of course, was not a religious leader; nevertheless, the value of religion was introduced into Iraqi propaganda as a powerful force around which Islamists could gather. President Bush countered the religious theme in his State of the Union speech (1/29/91) when he stated that "our" cause (the *we-they* dichotomy again) was just, moral, and right. Pope John Paul II described the war as "unworthy of humanity," but that note was lost in the polarized clash of persuasive messages between Islam and the West.

For propaganda to be completely successful, it must be linked to the de-sired effect of the message. For example, the Iraqi Scud missiles were used not only for direct military objectives, but also as a threatening message to Israel to provoke that country into a military response. The fact that Israel did not respond militarily to the Iraqi threat dulled the West's response to the propaganda and heightened a respect for Israel.

The most effective propaganda is generally based on fact, rather than a lie. The Iraqi Ministry of Information reported that Israeli aircraft were involved in air raids on Iraq. This claim was denied not only by Israel and the West, but also by the Saudis and the Syrians. This is an example of a domestic propaganda effort to influence Arab and Islamic opinion. Denial of a report by members of one's own group weakens the effect of the propaganda significantly.

Attack messages that appear ludicrous to the opponent will usually backfire. For example, *Baghdad Betty*, Iraqi radio broadcasting to U.S. troops, suggested that the soldiers' sweethearts back home were dating Tom Cruise, Bruce Willis, and even the cartoon character, Bart Simpson [reported in Britain's *Independent on Sunday* (2/25/91) and quoted in Taylor, 89-90]. This claim actually humored the American servicemen and was said to have bolstered their morale. Incidents such as this indicate that effective propaganda must be based on careful research of the enemy and knowledge of its culture. *Tokyo Rose* and *Lord Haw Haw*, in World War II, were more perceptive of their opponent's state of mind than was *Baghdad Betty*.

Disinformation can also be used as a subtle form of threat or domestic reinforcement of opinion and morale. Reports of casualties (ours and theirs), the number of airplanes shot down, the number of missiles fired, the number of prisoners taken, the number of civilian deaths frequently vary from one side to the other. Sometimes the discrepancies are considerable. But, one can also try to persuade through withholding information. If significant information is not reported, the picture of reality becomes distorted. For example, in the Gulf War, the Iraqis did not release any figures for the number of missing or captured troops. (The allies claimed 1,087.) The Iraqis also failed to report the number of Iraqi planes shot down. (The allies claimed 138.) The Iraqis also failed to report the number of Scuds fired. (The allies said that it was 61.) [report from the British *The Independent* (2/14/91), cited in Taylor, 132].

Purported communication within one's own organization (the military, in this instance) or information that is transmitted from a false source may be designed to deceive an enemy that is monitoring communications. For example, the Nazis used the technique of planting of information in opponents' publications to discredit the statements of opponents. Lies were placed in hostile newspapers that the Nazis would later deny with tangible evidence, thus discrediting the enemy's statements (Kris and Speier, 1945, 95). The purpose of this technique was to make the general public doubt the credibility of foreign news agencies and to disturb the relations between foreign newspapers and their agencies. Specifically, the Nazis would smuggle "material" and "announcements" into the hands of hostile news agencies in an effort to compromise these news representatives. In Germany, a clandestine anti-Nazi radio station, *Gustav Siegfried Eins*, was in operation. Its purpose was to undermine German public morale.

In the Gulf War, Baghdad radio would sometimes insert cryptic messages into its programming in an effort to deceive enemy monitors. Taylor (1998) quotes Britain's *Daily Telegraph* (2/6/91) and *The Times* (2/6/91) as saying things such as, "From the headquarters to Urwah: implement the last meeting" or "Call from Mahyub to 301: report to the bank" (133). Iraqi propaganda relied heavily on threats. After a while, however, the reliance on threats in propaganda depends upon whether the threats can be backed up by evidence.

For propaganda to be effective, it must use the full gamut of strategic objectives: the war aims of the nation, moral justification for one's actions (including the tapping of core values), and support by the domestic population. The Gulf War saw very different approaches being used by the two sides. The conflict was between Judeo-Christian values and the Islamic concept of *jihad*. This easily explains the frequent comparison made to the Crusades.

Propaganda aimed primarily at domestic audiences lays the groundwork for future action and provides a rationalized blanket to cushion the impact on the domestic audience of the unpleasant, imminent action. The most effective propaganda will also arouse the passions of the domestic audience by calling forth their stored concepts of patriotism, democracy, and national unity. The interest in self-defense and self-protection are often a part of the emotional mix. Immediately preceding the Gulf War, then President (George H. W.) Bush and the American Secretary of State, James Baker, realized that the American people needed to be prepared for something more than a series of neat, surgical air strikes. Ground troops would have to be used and in fairly substantial numbers. The propaganda themes of both Bush and Baker included the idea that the objective of war would be total victory in a just war being fought against a brutal dictator. The two leaders stressed that everything possible would be done to limit civilian casualties and even indicated what the first steps would be in American post-war policy. Therefore, a kind, caring American democracy was pitted against a murderous, evil totalitarianism. Such major core value clashes don't need to be stated as such. The value components are often hidden inside the attack mechanism and may be detected by implication.

A second core value used in the Bush/Baker propaganda statements was humanitarianism. Humanistic values of Americanism were pitted against ruthless, self-serving interests of the totalitarians, whose disrespect for life allowed the enemy to murder without compunction. One needs to be aware, of course, that the values ascribed to the enemy are those designed by the American propagandists. Designed from the other side, the core values referred to would be defined very differently. However, creating value dichotomies—good versus evil, God versus the devil, compassion versus tyranny—makes the persuasive attacks simpler to understand and integrates the emotion related to the idea into the receiver's composite response. The emotion inside the idea gives the idea power and creates a will in the receiver.

American propaganda aims in the Gulf War were short-range, because America had planned on a short war. Iraqi television broadcast the images of the carnage caused by the bombing directly to the Islamic world in time for the evening news. Among the allies, a substantial amount of self-censorship occurred, similar to the way local television crews would photograph a severe auto accident or a car-train crash. The Vietnam War Syndrome has had a considerable influence on the way that the American military and the media interact regarding shocking close-ups of mutilated bodies or of body bags of American servicemen being flown home. Many American military personnel believe that images such as these, which were used more freely in Vietnam, were a major cause of resistance to the war at home. Of course, what one doesn't show in a picture may define the image as much as what one does show.

The Iraqi images were framed differently from those sent through the information limitations observed by the West. Iraqi television often showed the grizzly images of death and destruction. The verbal images, used in headlines in this instance, drew upon the stored values in the Islamic states supporting Iraq and reflected the outrage felt from the shock of an attack. A similar outrage occurred in America as a result of the coordinated airliner attack on the twin towers of the World Trade Center in New York (9/11/01).

In Tunisia, the headlines shouted "Shame on them," "Carnage," "Massacre," "Barbaric Butchery." In Lebanon, the press ran stories about "an American massacre in Baghdad." The Algerian president said that the war appeared to be one of "extermination" (report by CNN, 2/14/91). In the Arab coalition countries, however, the reaction to the American attack was directed primarily at Saddam Hussein. The vivid use of pictures by the Iraqis generated an overall image in the Islamic world of Iraq as a victim rather than an aggressor. As noted previously, the image of victimization is a puissant propaganda tool, in the opposite sense of an image of all-encompassing brutal power about to be unleashed. Sympathy and terror are both potent persuasive messages.

The American-led coalition had demonstrated that it not only controlled the battlefield, but also that it controlled much of the world's communication systems and news organizations. As Taylor (1998) says,

> During the war, Iraqi propaganda had made a great play of the "vile", "hypocritical", and "atheistic" influence of the United States in the region, which

was being achieved with the connivance of the oil-rich Gulf Arab states—and
this clearly hit a chord in Middle Eastern streets. Interestingly, American black
propaganda also exploited these themes as a way of encouraging Iraqis to over-
throw Saddam. (266)

Incidentally, "white" propaganda is overt and based on information. "Black"
propaganda appears to be coming from someplace that it is not. In the Gulf
War, for example, black broadcasts appeared to be coming from transmitters
within areas controlled by the coalition. Special forces units operated behind
enemy lines and set up transmitters close to enemy troop emplacements and
cities. Those transmitters then broadcast "voices of disaffection." Coalition
propagandists hoped that an apparent upsurge against Saddam Hussein would
encourage listeners to lose morale and think about defecting.

Despite the large number of reporters in the Middle East, most had to rely
on military briefings for much of their information. The result of this was that
an essentially unified image of the war appeared in the Western press. Taylor
(1998) says, "It was monopoly in the guise of pluralism" (268). With a few
exceptions, the American and British media were largely uncritical and supported the official assessment of the progress of the war.

Two specific propaganda themes during the war were shown later to have
been distorted. The first was the coalition's success in eliminating Iraq's nuclear program; the second concerned the general accuracy of allied bombing.
Censorship was confined almost entirely to military strategy and operations.
Censorship of beliefs and convictions was rare. Because most of the media
supported the Western beliefs and values, there was little need to censor beliefs and values.

Reporting from journalists embedded with allied coalition units has advan-
tages and disadvantages. The advantage is that the television viewer can get
a glimpse of some activity on the spot. The disadvantage is that the view of
the war is seen from a very narrow perspective, and that can result in image
distortion. As this author notes in *Ethnic Media in America* (2004), the vista
provided by the camera (or the descriptive narrative of the reporter's pen) is
equivalent to that of a carpenter ant on a sequoia tree. Asked to define the tree,
the ant would describe the long, parallel mountain ridges and deep crevasses
around him, occasionally obfuscated by shadows of huge green canopies. The
ant's report might be completely accurate and objective, but it would provide
an inaccurate idea of what a sequoia tree is like from a human perspective (17).
Providing various images of the war from journalists in different locations allows the viewer (or reader) to assemble the various images; nevertheless, all of
the parts don't provide an image or understanding of the event as a whole.

Planning and implementing propaganda is as important as planning and
implementing military logistical activities. This is especially true if propa-

ganda is going to appear as something other than propaganda. It must be a covert activity, as intelligence is. In the Gulf War, propaganda was employed heavily on both sides. The Western coalition stressed that this was a "just war," and it personified the conflict in the form of Saddam Hussein and the Republican Guard rather than in the form of the Iraqi people.

A final point, made by Taylor (1998), concerns the journalistic expectation that the public has a right to know about events. However,

> As for the role of journalists as custodians of the public's right to know, the Gulf War has presented a new challenge: the public's apparent desire *not* to know beyond the sketchiest details what is going on while it is going on. Whereas journalists see speed as essential to their profession, their readers seemed more than willing to wait until the military could report that a mission had been accomplished before finding out about it. (274)

Some competing value systems have been discussed in previous chapters. In thinking about propaganda as a strategy, one should have an understanding of one's own values (American, if it is propaganda from an American perspective, British, if it is propaganda from a British perspective, etc.) With a comprehensive list and solid understanding of one's own values, one can then construct a corresponding list of the values of the target audience. From that point on, similarities and differences can be defined and strengths and weaknesses of each system can be determined. That should then suggest the thesis for one's persuasive message.

From an American perspective, one should categorize and define the American value/belief system. This author will mention a few core values here, but this is not intended to be an exhaustive list. It is offered as a guide, a starting point for prospective persuasive activity. The American political structure of *representative democracy* (balance in government) is a core value and is the pillar of the American democratic system. The word *republicanism* is often used for this general value. This value entails government by the people through periodic free elections, power that is exercised by the people directly or indirectly. This entails the rule of the majority; this ensures that the supreme power resides in the hands of the people. The tripartite form of government (the executive branch, the legislative branch, and the judicial branch) is intended to provide a balanced consideration of the divergent interests of the American population.

The second core value is *liberalism* and encompasses several values that may be defined as core values in themselves. Liberalism is a political theory founded on the natural goodness of humans and the autonomy of the individual. Liberalism favors civil and political liberties, government by law with the consent of the governed, and protection from arbitrary authority. Elements of liberalism are often thought of as separate core values themselves. One of those elements is the *rule of law*. This value assures against the assumption of power by a dictator. This value reverses the tradition in many societies of rule by a strongman. *Individualism* is a second element that is often identified as a distinct core value. Individualism involves a belief in the primary importance of the individual and in the virtues of self-reliance and personal independence.

American capitalism includes the core value of *consumerism*. This "shop-until-you-drop" principle recognizes the importance of buying as an essential ingredient in the economy's financial stability. *Materialism* is part of the capitalistic mix. Social status and power are associated with the number and value of material possessions.

Education is a core value. Knowledge and skill development may be considered a value in itself but are more often thought of as a tool for gainful employment. However, a cynical trend seems to be shifting the value of knowledge and skill for their own sake, or for a constructive contribution to society through employment, management, or entrepreneurial business, to achievement of formal certification (however achieved), which tends to vitiate the true significance of education.

Egalitarianism has become a fundamental value in America and is an example of how values can change with time and new circumstances. Equality is the central theme of egalitarianism, which affirms, promotes, and is characterized by belief in equal political, economic, social, and civil rights for all people. This principle may help explain the desire of many people to champion the underdog in competition if no particular fan relationship exists on one side or the other. Egalitarianism expresses a desire for fairness and balance in outcomes.

A value that might be termed *cultural determinism* lies at the heart of entertainment in the United States. According to this principle, cultural matters are determined by popular taste, and popular taste largely governs the type of music that is produced, the types of movies that are made, the types of television dramatic series that are aired, and even much of the content of news. What becomes popular with most people is that which drives the production of entertainment.

The final value mentioned here is not one that this author has cited elsewhere; yet, it is a value that has important ramifications for communication. It is a value that might be called *unidimensional communication*. That value is characterized by unambiguity in interpersonal communication. It is characterized by the cowboy slogans "I say what I mean, and I mean what I say" and "I shoot from the hip." This principle is economical in time in a communication interchange; this principle also suggests personal integrity (I'm honest, straightforward, and can be trusted). I don't speak to deceive.

In contrast, in Eastern Europe and the Russian Federation, university colleagues told this author that there is an expectation that interpersonal communication may exist at three levels—not one. This is not to say that communication always occurs at three levels but that one should approach interpersonal communication with that expectation. A three-level expectation produces *tridimensional communication*. The idea is that "I might say one thing; I might mean something else; and I might do something quite different." The *meaning* and the *action* may be similar to each other or quite different. The point is that a tridimensional level of communication provides a sliding scale between point (1) "I might say one thing," and point (2) "I might mean something different [It might be similar to what one says or very different from what was said in step (1)]. Step (2) reflects the unspoken meaning behind the statement in step (1), and step (3) implies that the resulting action might not reflect exactly what was said in step (1) or what was meant in step (2) " I might do something quite different" from what I suggested the action would be in steps (1) and (2). The intent in unidimensional communication, immediately, is to convey accurate meaning, veracity, and integrity. The unidimensional code suggests complete integrity reflected in the first statement.

The tridimensional form of communication provides a more intriguing verbal interchange. It involves trying to read the other person's mind while listening to the words. A female Russian colleague once said, "Western men are so naïve. They take at face value what a woman says" (not cited to protect the person's identity). This was not a gender-oriented statement and should not be taken to assume that such a view is limited to females. This was a statement about communication levels, and it applies to men in certain contexts as well. Men also use communication, with a flexible range between statement, meaning, and action, in some countries where barter or sales are dependent upon a flexible range between statement, meaning, and action. This can range from an open-air market in the Middle East to a boardroom in Moscow. Incidentally, it is not uncommon in totalitarian countries, where freedom of speech is limited and speech may be punished, for communicators to obscure the meaning of their statements intentionally for self-protection, and the practice of obfuscation in dialogue may be traced to experience under a totalitarian regime.

PRACTICAL PROPAGANDA TECHNIQUES

This work is not intended to be a handbook on propaganda technique that might be applied as a template for the propagandist. Nevertheless, an overview of some of the Psychological Operations (PSYOPS) suggestions in the

U.S. Army field manual on propaganda might provide an insight into the ways that some of the general principles of propaganda have been discussed in previous chapters. The following section will follow the listing of techniques as developed in the field manual. An explanation of those techniques will usually draw upon ideas presented previously in this book.

The Army field manual stresses the importance of planning, development, and message dissemination possibilities so that the techniques used will fit the objectives of the propaganda campaign. Therefore, analysis of the enemy's values, interests, needs, and concerns are important at the top level of psychological operations campaigns (where long-range objectives are desired). Short-range field objectives may be more limited in the psychological methods used to bring about immediate action—fear, demoralization, strategic plan deception, and a self-fulfilling prophecy (You are going to lose anyway. You might as well give up now).

The Army places techniques in five categories: (1) characteristics of the content self-evident, (2) additional information required to be recognized, (3) evident only after extended output, (4) nature of the arguments used, and (5) inferred intent of the originator (cited in Appendix I: PSYOP Techniques. Department of the Army. 1).

Self-evident techniques are those in which the receiver of the message is able to recognize the meaning or to conjure up an image from the word or phrase itself. Name-calling and slogans are examples of this technique. Other self-evident techniques may include an *appeal to authority*. If a prominent person endorses a particular idea, argument, or course of action, the sense of authority vested in that person has persuasive impact in itself. Assumptions are made about a person in authority. The person is knowledgeable, powerful, a problem solver, and has the interests of his constituents at heart.

An *assertion* may be made as a self-evident technique. An assertion consists of a positive statement, without supporting evidence, that is made on the assumption that the receiver of the message will accept the statement at face value. Actually, assertions may or may not be true.

A *get-on-the-bandwagon* appeal can be an effective self-evident technique. Social acceptability is a powerful motivating force, and the desire to be an accepted member of a social group that is headed toward "victory" provides a sense of fulfillment. People usually want to be on the winning side.

In the *obtain disapproval* technique, the propagandist's objective is to link a particular action or idea to a group that is hated, feared, or held in contempt. If the enemy embraces a particular idea or activity, the tendency of one's own group is to distance itself from the enemy by actively strengthening one's attitude in favor of the opposing view, thus creating a more clearly defined and vigorous opposition of viewpoints.

Glittering generalities involve words and phrases that tap the value/belief system of the adaptive unconscious—words such as "our country," "home," "peace," "freedom," and "honor." The glittering generality is an easy and effective device to use, but one must be careful to assure that the frame of reference is the same each time that a glittering generality is used. If the frame of reference changes, different words or phrases may need to be chosen. The generalities are intentionally *vague* so that the receiver of the message can fill in his own meaning. The principle of the mosaic, discussed previously, is applicable here. If the receiver of the message has to commit some of his own thought or impressions into a message to fill in the blanks, that generally unconscious work gives the receiver a sense of having participated in the creation of the message. That sense of participation gives the receiver a feeling of partial ownership of the message, and we usually embrace what we own.

Rationalization functions in a manner similar to the vagueness of glittering generalities. Favorable generalities may be used to rationalize questionable actions or beliefs and, therefore, confirm unreasoned opinions or beliefs.

Favorable generalities usually involve *simplification*. Most receivers won't go to the trouble to apply a rational analysis of the idea contained in a message. Simplification of wording, image, and idea will allow the receiver to embrace or deny the content of a message immediately, without having to go through a convoluted, analytical thought process.

Transfer of a positive or negative quality (praise or blame) of a person, entity, or value to another person, entity, or value is to make the object of the transfer more acceptable or discredited. This process may refer to a person, an organization, a nation, or a belief, such as patriotism. A message designed with this objective in mind is intended to generate an emotional response which stimulates the target audience to identify with recognized authorities and, therefore, to align the receiver of the message more closely with the interests, beliefs, and objectives of the authorities.

What the military calls the *least of evils* (but which might better be known as *comparative advantage*) refers to a situation where the generator of the message (the propagandist) admits that none of the plans being proposed is perfect. They all have some disadvantages, but the plan being proposed by the propagandist is the best among the alternatives (or, perhaps, the least of evils).

Name-calling or substitutions of names or moral labels taps the prejudices and stereotypes of an audience by labeling the message receiver as something that the target audience fears, loathes, or finds personally distasteful. *Direct* name-calling is effective when the audience is sympathetic or neutral. The name used associates the derogatory image of the characteristics in the called name with that of the person's real name. *Indirect* name-calling is a subtle use of this disparaging device when direct name-calling might antagonize the target audience. Sarcasm and ridicule are examples of this device. Satire is an effective way of disparaging the object of the satire. Satire is usually sophisticated and often subtle, but the effect of satire can have a long-term neutralizing effect on the message receiver. *Cartoons, illustrations, and photographs* may be used with deadly effect and have been at the heart of most propaganda campaigns. The caricature of a person is simple, direct, generates humor, and leaves a powerful lasting image. The caution in using this device is that remarks made by insiders of a group will seem acceptable, whereas the same remark made by an outsider might seem objectionable. People will often provide sharp criticism of people or events in their own country but feel defensive if those remarks come from someone from another country or from someone outside of their social circle.

Pinpointing the enemy is a form of simplification and defines the enemy clearly so that a sharp image is formed in the receiver's mind. That image can be evoked for an accusation. Country X's troops had to move into the two provinces to protect the population of those areas from genocide by Country Y.

Plain folks or common man is a propaganda technique that suggests that we are all ordinary people who have interests, problems, and desires in common. The common man has "common" sense and, therefore, can be appealed to with arguments that seem to have an inherent logic to ordinary people like us. In face-to-face communication, or in mediated visual communication, the propagandist should dress, talk, and behave in a manner that would not make the propagandist stand apart from members of the target audience.

Variations on the plain folks theme include *presenting soldiers as plain folks*. The propagandist wants the enemy soldier who has one of your own soldiers in his rifle sight to visualize a person like himself, rather than a "bloodthirsty" killer, before he pulls the trigger. The soldier should be made to look like a "decent" person. It may be just as important—or even more important—for the propagandist to make one's own *civilians appear as plain folks*. The plain folks theme for the civilian population is intended to dispel the impression among the enemy that your population consists of arrogant, immoral, warmongering people. Instead, we are people who, like you, want to live at peace. *Humanizing leaders* is another subcategory of the plain folks theme. This objective paints one's own leaders as wise, thoughtful, and kind—something of a father figure.

Several devices can be used to enhance the effectiveness of the *plain folks* theme. These devices make the message seem to be coming from someone with similar knowledge, values, and lifestyles. The propaganda strategist also has to ask whether use of plain-folk devices would undermine the credibility of the source. A decision there would depend on a careful examination of the objective of the message. Plain folk devices include use of the vernacular in communication—the language, songs, idioms, and jokes that are common to a specific region. Consistency in *dialect* with residents of a certain area will make the propagandist's message seem to fit in with the linguistic expectations of the target group. Dialect refers to a variation in pronunciation, grammar, and vocabulary from regional or national norms. Intentional *errors* built into a scholastic or formally trained speech style can make the communication seem spontaneous, thus more natural, and thus more acceptable to plain folks. *Homey words* present a comfortable, rosy image to the listener and tend to dull the edge of hostility among the audience. Examples of such words are "home," "family," "children," "farm," "neighbors," and other words that would fit the cultural context of the audience.

Social disapproval (or ostracism) is an effective technique if there is an opportunity to demonstrate that certain attitudes, opinions, or actions would result in disapproval by the group as a whole and thus result in social rejection by the group. Social acceptance by one's group is strong glue. Ostracism is a common control practice used by peer groups and tribal societies.

What military propagandists call *virtue words* (positive words that create a favorable image of the person to whom the words are applied) are used to create a sense of security in the target audience and trust in the authorities to which the words are attached. The specific words chosen need to work in concert to create the particular image that the propagandist wants to create. Virtue words include words such as "wise and firm leadership," "peace," "happiness," and "freedom."

A *slogan* taps the adaptive unconscious directly and constitutes a good example of activating a stereotype. A slogan is a brief phrase that taps a stereotype. A memorable slogan is effective because it encapsulates the essence of a person or thing and can be used in exactly the same form for a long time. Recruitment slogans used by the U.S. Army consist, among others, of "Be all that you can be—in the Army," and, simply, "Army strong."

Testimonials used in military propaganda usually refer to one of the two types of evidence used in persuasion in general—expert testimony. In this case, opinions are sought from experts in a particular discipline. The expert's knowledge, understanding, and experience in the field gives his opinion greater weight than would be given to the opinion of a layman in the field. *Expert testimony* in a propaganda message is intended to draw the attitudes and opinions of members of the target audience to those of the expert. The magnet for this attraction is the respect invested in the authority. The respect comes from *accomplishment*, an authority that has demonstrated outstanding proficiency in his field. *Identification with the target* eases the process of vicarious identification between the target audience and the speaker (or writer).

БУДЬ НА ЧЕКУ,
В ТАКИЕ ДНИ
ПОДСЛУШИВАЮТ СТЕНЫ.
НЕДАЛЕКО ОТ БОЛТОВНИ
И СПЛЕТНИ
ДО ИЗМЕНЫ.

НЕ БОЛТАЙ!

Figure 6.1. Propaganda (in this case, advice) is often directed at one's own citizenry. This poster of a strong, determined, concerned young woman admonishes the Soviet citizens to be careful about what they say in public. Speech is punishable. Verbal dissent undermines the strength of one's political cause and impedes the formation of uniform thought that undergirds the philosophy of a political movement. The inscription on the poster says, "These days, even walls can hear you. Chatting and gossiping are but one step away from treason. Don't chatter!"

The military may be a common bond between a member of the target audience and the authority. A soldier is likely to identify more easily with a senior military officer who has shared some common experience with the soldier than he would be likely to identify with a civilian. One's position of authority may instill confidence in the testimony. Of course, a group's negative reaction to an authority's action over time may also result in a degradation of the sense of trust in the originator of the message. The propagandist needs to be sensitive to the public perception of the authority that is used.

Likening one thing to another (in the form of a metaphor or simile), or *inanimate objects,* is often associating the quality of some *thing* with some *person*—solid as the Rock of Gibraltar, swift as a deer, he leaped like a kangaroo (similes), his mind is a keen-edged knife (metaphor). (A simile consists of a comparison of dissimilar things, using *like* or *as*. A metaphor consists of an implied comparison of dissimilar things, not using *like* or *as*.) The direct comparison used in a metaphor is more jarring than the indirect comparison of a simile and, therefore, is somewhat more powerful than the simile. Expert testimony may be used effectively if one can get a statement from an *enemy leader* that condemns some aspect of enemy policy or behavior. The enemy target audience usually values the statements of authoritative leaders.

A second kind of testimony used in argument is *lay testimony.* This testimony involves a description of an event experienced by an observer who may not be an expert in the field in question. A person standing at the intersection of two busy streets might coincidentally witness a traffic accident. A policeman investigating the incident moments later might ask the bystander to describe what he saw. His description of the event at the accident site constitutes lay testimony. The bystander might not be a crime expert, but he was a direct observer of a significant event. His common-man description of the accident could even be used in court. That raises a verbal description of an event (at times including an opinion) to a high level of importance. The principle of lay testimony may be applied somewhat indirectly in the military to *fellow soldiers* as personal sources of testimonial authority. Soldiers often have common experiences in the military and tend to respect the opinion of their fellow soldiers. In addition to getting testimonial evidence from opposing military leaders, testimonial evidence from *opposing leaders* (civilian leaders) may also carry authoritative weight. *Famous scholars, writers, and other personalities* (including scientists and commentators) may also be used in propaganda messages in much the same way as one would use messages from other authorities (expert testimony).

Audio-visual devices may include symbols that reinforce a message and constitute something of a testimonial. Examples would be the use of flags on a podium behind a speaker, *The Battle Hymn of the Republic* as the music bed of a patriotic video, the arrangement of a president and his cabinet members for a group photo opportunity—the president in the middle, the other officers, essentially in rank order, displayed to the right and left, or a general speaking in uniform rather than civilian clothes. To be credible, testimonials must seem plausible to the receiver of the message, and it should be a true statement. A false testimonial may easily be discredited, which reflects negatively on the reliability of the propagandist.

Propaganda techniques are often concerned with the content of a message and how the content can be used to direct the receiver's attention and guide his emotional response. One of these techniques is what the military calls *incredible truths*. There may be times when an unbelievable event has occurred, details of which have been kept secret from the enemy's populace, or when the enemy has glossed over an event that would damage its cause. For example, if Country X is at war with Country Y, and unbeknownst to Country X, Country Y is about ready to declare war against Country X, this might constitute an incredible truth that could be used in propaganda messages to the enemy.

A *double-cutting edge* consists of an argument (however formulated) that does double duty by simultaneously bolstering one's own position while denigrating that of the opposition. A common term for this device is a *double-edged sword*.

Insinuation involves suggestions that certain negative characteristics apply to the enemy nation, groups, or individuals. Although fact is implied, no proof is offered, just suspicion created through allusion. The uncertainty associated with the idea in an insinuation resembles the uncertainty that is characteristic of a rumor. A negative idea conjured up in the mind of the receiver pushes the emotion toward anxiety. In a positive insinuation, the receiver is again driven toward a certain anxiety—this time one of possible false hope. Examples of potentially divisive insinuation might consist of focusing on political divisions between the enemy and its allies, or focusing on the powerlessness of the individual. This theme could be used to dissociate the target audience's interests and concerns from the contrary policies of the government.

Seven insinuation techniques are cited in the U.S. Army's *Propaganda Techniques* manual. One may use *leading questions*, questions that allow for only one answer, an answer that is built into the design of the question. For example, "What is your unit to do now that it is surrounded and cut off?" The only reasonable answer? Surrender.

Logical structures closely related to leading questions are *begging the question* and *loaded questions*. In begging the question, the proposition to be proved is assumed implicitly or explicitly in one of the premises. One might say that, "The *insidious* propaganda of the Communist Party should be condemned." Regardless of whether the question is answered in the affirmative or the negative, the response links the idea of *insidious* to *propaganda*. A *loaded question* is a question with a false or questionable presupposition, and it is loaded with that presumption. One condemns oneself one way or another regardless of how one answers the question. The classic example is, "Have you stopped beating your wife lately?"

Humor can be an effective form of insinuation. Jokes and cartoons provoke a readier response than do logically constructed arguments. *Pure motives* makes it clear that the purveyor of the message (the propagandist) is acting in the best interest of the target audience, whereas the enemy (perhaps the government of an opposing regime, as opposed to the general population) is acting in a manner contrary to the best interest of the target audience. *Guilt by association* links a person, group, or idea to another person, group, or idea and suggests that the association in itself demonstrates like-mindedness of the two entities. For example, "Senator X had a meeting with Communist Party member Y. Therefore, Senator X must be a Communist sympathizer."

Rumor is a form of insinuation. Rumors tend to create anxiety, because the factual outcome of the insinuated event can't be known at the time. *Pictorial and photographic propaganda* is insinuation that conveys idea and feeling directly, without having to have the mind translate words into images and emotions. *Vocal inflection* may be used to suggest a derogatory notion, such as sarcasm or ridicule.

When one chooses facts, ideas, and opinions selectively to advance one's case, one is engaged in *card stacking* or *selective omission*. This simply involves putting one's best foot forward. This is the technique referred to in public relations as *spin*. Spin should not include falsification, but does include taking true statements and images and juxtaposing them so that they cast the most favorable light possible on the person, organization, or cause. In essence, the propagandist selects the most favorable true facts and images and advances them as his argument. This construction of facts and images is presented as the basis for drawing conclusions.

If opposing arguments are understood and given some credence by the opposition, the propagandist may want to acknowledge that argument and present a counterargument, a term that the military calls *presenting the other side*. With some audiences, presenting as irrefutable an argument on one side or the other may seem disingenuous, and the audience will question the credibility of the communicator. In that case, agreeing with minor aspects of the enemy's point of view may be an effective introduction to an argument, with the progression of your argument demonstrating the comparative advantage of your proposal in comparison with that of your opponent.

Propaganda is often associated with lies and distortion—*lying and distortion*, in military terminology. Although bald-faced lies have sometimes been used in propaganda, they should be avoided, not only on ethical terms, but also on very practical terms. An out-and-out lie can often be exposed as such, and when a liar is exposed, his credibility evaporates. Distortion should be distinguished from spin. Spin is like digital enhancement of a photograph. The image on the photograph is a representation of a real person or object or a digitized construction of an idea. *Distortion* transforms an image that has reality in one context to a context of totally different type. If that context difference is not cited, a totally false image is presented. That distortion falls in the category of a lie.

Occam's razor tells us that if we are considering various theories about a particular thing, the simplest of the theories should be preferred. By simplification, the theory means that all extraneous or irrelevant elements in a theory should be eliminated. Simplification is an important activity and something to be encouraged in any analytical process. Albert Einstein (1933) advocated simplifying theory as far as it will go. Einstein may be paraphrased as saying, "Everything should be made as simple as possible, but not simpler" (Einstein, Web, Quotes).

This maxim is applicable to the military propagandist's technique of *simplification*. The military's advice is to simplify interpretations of events, ideas, concepts, or personalities. Statements should be positive and firm, without qualifying words. Simplification provides simple solutions for complex problems. Simple statements largely bypass the "troublesome" problem of mental analysis of a more complex statement. Meaning and connotation are nearly instantaneous. Simplification implies that the communicator is going to the heart of the matter in a few words; it also suggests that the communicator has such a good understanding of the subject that he is able to condense a complex idea into a simple statement. Nevertheless, the wise propagandist will heed the advice in Occam's razor. For a statement to appear credible, it should not be simplified beyond credulity. *Stereotyping* is also a device used by propagandists. As mentioned throughout this book, stereotyping is effective because it taps preconceived concepts and emotions that lie in the adaptive unconscious mind.

When considering a composite message strategy over time, three propaganda techniques are often used. The first technique is *change of pace,* a switch that involves reversing the tone of a series of messages. This might involve going from belligerent to peaceful, from "hot" to "cold," from gloomy prophecy to optimism, from emotion to fact. The second technique is *stalling*. If an event is occurring which could bring about a sharp, negative reaction, the propagandist may withhold information on the topic until the passion of the moment has subsided. The assumption is that a likely negative outburst will be muted. The third technique involves a *shift of scene*. This technique involves changing the subject. By shifting the focus from one aspect of an event to another—or from one story to another—the propagandist hopes to decrease interest in the inflammatory event or story by shifting the audience's attention to a less inflammatory event or story.

Advertisers know the importance of *repetition* in their messages. The same text, jingle, and image may even be run back to back within the same program, or the text and music packaged for radio as an additional way of reinforcing the advertiser's message. Habitual use of a skill or a value is not only the way that we learn something, but also it is a way of making the skill or value permanent. When we learn to walk, the repetition of that activity sets the skill in our unconscious mind so that we don't have to think through all of the progressive steps each time we stand up. Learning and storing purchase prompts is similar; so is learning and storing values. The technique of repetition is also of considerable importance to the propagandist. Repetition calls the image and associated emotion to the conscious mind, and, with repetition, the ease with which that transformation from the unconscious to the conscious mind becomes like the now-automatic series of procedures that we use in walking.

Homeostasis is an important dynamic in the human psyche, because it acts as a force resisting the inevitable change that occurs over time. The propagandist refers to this characteristic as *fear of change*. If people have become comfortable with a certain lifestyle or pattern of behavior, a sudden, forced change from without that disturbs the psychological equilibrium generates fear. If people are comfortable with their status, wealth, friendship circles, or safety, they will resist a program that might change any of these elements. The advice to the propagandist, in this regard, is that a psychological campaign must give the members of the audience a safe, honorable way to change without damaging their sense of self and position in their environment.

A powerful propaganda technique involves exposure of *terrorism*. Official United States policy is opposed to the use of terrorism or terror tactics. However, exposing terror used by the enemy may be a force in creating repugnance toward the groups using terror tactics. Propaganda campaigns that expose terror may be used with the general populace of the country sponsoring terrorist groups. Most people, even in these countries, find terror tactics repulsive. Exposure of terrorist activities is also effective in neutral countries, because the savagery of the act creates fear in the minds of those people through vicarious identification with the victims of terror. The enemy may try to rationalize his terrorist activity on the basis of the principle that the end justifies the means, but the imagery and sounds of terrorist actions will override the rationalized counterpropaganda by the enemy in the minds of most people. Imagery that evokes a deep emotion, such as fear, will assume more significance in the minds of people than a logical rationalization of the reason for use of terror tactics.

Except for survival itself, speech (in all of its forms, whether spoken or written) is of utmost importance, because language as speech is the tool that allows the will of man to bring about the constant evolution of society. As the German author Thomas Mann wrote, "Speech is civilization itself. The words, even the most contradictory word, preserves contact—it is silence which isolates" (518).

REFERENCES

Aristotle. The rhetoric of Aristotle. Trans. James Edward Cowell Weldon, 1886. London: Macmillan Elibron Classics reprint. Adamant Media 2005. http://www .elibron.com

Bush, George H.W. 2005. State of the union address. 1991, January 29. In *George H.W. Bush: Speeches of the 41st president.* [DVD]. Amazon.com.

Caricature. 2007. *Wikipedia, the free encyclopedia,* March. Accessed December 15, 2008, from http://en.wikipedia.org/wiki/caricature.

CNN. [Television broadcast]. 1991, February 14. Cable News Network.

Daily Telegraph [U.K.]. 1991, January 7.

Daily Telegraph [U.K.]. 1991, February 6.

DeFleur, Melvin L, and Sandra J. Ball-Rokeach. 1989. *Theories of mass communication* (5th ed.). New York: Longman.

Edwards, Allen Louis. 1940. Studies of stereotypes, I: The directionality and uniformity of response to stereotypes. *The Journal of Social Psychology,* 12, 357-366.

Einstein, Albert. 1993. Web, Quotes. 2008, May 20. Accessed December 29, 2008, from http://equotes.wetpaint.com/page/Albert+Einstein+Quotes?t=anon.

Fairness and Accuracy in Reporting (FAIR). 2008. VisualWikipedia.com. [a progressive media criticism organization based in New York City, founded in 1986]. Accessed December 15, 2008 from http://visualwikipedia.com/en/Fairness_and_Accuracy_in_Reporting.

Guardian [U.K.]. 1991, January 18.

The Independent [U.K.]. 1991, January 28.

The Independent [U.K.]. 1991, February 14.

Kris, Ernst, and Hans Speier. 1944. *German radio propaganda: Report on home broadcasts during the war.* New York: Oxford University Press.

Lippmann, Walter. 1922. *Public opinion.* New York: The Free Press.

Mann, Thomas. 1927. *The magic mountain.* Trans. Helen Tracy Lowe-Porter. New York: Alfred A. Knoph, Vintage Books Edition, March 1969.

Ortega y Gasset, J. 1932. *The revolt of the masses.* Trans. anon. New York: W.W. Norton. First published in Spanish in 1930.

Pope John Paul II. 1991. Quotes. Accessed December 29, 2008, from www.antiwar .com/quotes.php.

Propaganda Techniques, 1979 August. Based on *Appendix I, PSYOP techniques,* from *Psychological operations field manual,* No. 33-1. Washington, DC: Head-quarters, Department of the Army. Accessed November 29, 2008, from http://www.zoehouse.com/is/sco/proptech.html.

Rauschning, Hermann. 1940. *The voice of destruction.* New York: G.P. Putnam's Sons.

Renz, Byron B. 2004. Theoretical foundation underlying minority group and media interaction. In Meiss and Tait, eds. *Ethnic media in America,* Bk. 3. Dubuque, IA: Kendall/Hunt.

Taylor, Philip M. 1998). *War and the media: Propaganda and persuasion in the Gulf War,* 2nd ed. Manchester: University Press.

The Times [U.K.] 1991, January 23.

The Times [U.K.] 1991, January 28.

The Times [U.K.] 1991, February 6.

Tönnies, Ferdinand. 1957. *Community and Society (Gemeinschaft und Gesellschaft).* Charles P. Loomis, trans. and ed. East Lansing, MI: Michigan State University Press. First published in German in 1887.

Index

www.ingramcontent.com/pod-product-compliance
Lightning Source LLC
Chambersburg PA
CBHW030810280326
41926CB00085B/437